Gamification and Design Thinking in Higher Education

This book analyzes the use of gamification and design thinking in higher education, examining how both techniques can be combined and used together to promote motivation, engagement, and participation among students.

Using two in-depth examples, the authors show that the introduction of a gamified design in a design thinking activity can be a powerful tool to enhance the experiences of students in the teaching-learning process of a subject; motivate participants in a design thinking activity in the university environment; and enhance skills such as creativity, critical thinking and problem-solving, and collaboration, widely demanded in the labor market. Further, they examine how gamification and design thinking in the educational field can enable both the motivation and engagement of students and promote behavioral changes that materialize as a boost in learning outcomes and academic performance.

Providing valuable recommendations and insights into the analysis, design and development, and implementation and evaluation of gamified design thinking activities to be carried out in higher education, as well as examining relevant ethical issues, the book will appeal to scholars, researchers, academic faculty, and educators working in the field of higher education, and with interests in educational psychology and theories of learning.

Carmen Bueno Muñoz is Lecturer at the Department of Economics, the Faculty of Economics and Business, the University of Zaragoza, Spain. She has a Ph.D. from the University of Extremadura, Spain, and was granted the Extraordinary Doctorate Award from the same university.

Núria Hernández Nanclares is Associate Professor at the Department of Applied Economics, University of Oviedo, Spain. She holds a Ph.D. in economics and is specialized in teaching innovation in economics and higher education. She is accredited for online teaching by the University of Oviedo, Spain, and as a "Flipped Learning" trainer by the Flipped Learning Global Initiative (FLGI).

Luis R. Murillo Zamorano is Associate Professor at the Department of Economics and Director of the Research Group in Economic Analysis and Marketing Management (AEDIMARK R&D Group) in the University of Extremadura, Spain. He has a Ph.D. in economics from the University of York, UK.

José Ángel López Sánchez is Associate Professor in the Marketing and Market Research Area and Researcher in the Research Group on Economic Analysis and Marketing Management (AEDIMARK R&D Group) in the University of Extremadura, Spain. He has a Ph.D. from the University of Oviedo, Spain.

Routledge Research in Higher Education

Accommodating Marginalized Students in Higher Education
A Structural Theory Approach
WP Wahl and Louis H. Falik

The Evolving Nature of Universities
What Shapes and Influences Identity in International Higher Education
Edited by Judith Lamie and Christopher Hill

Emancipatory Human Rights and the University
Promoting Social Justice in Higher Education
Edited by Felisa Tibbitts and André Keet

Universities in Times of Crisis and Disruption
Dislocated Complexity
Lorraine Ling and Kay Livingston

Developing a Model for Culturally Responsive Experiential Education
Teachers as Allies in Student Journeys of Decolonization
Elizabeth Laura Hope Yomantas

Creating Supportive Spaces for Pregnant and Parenting College Students
Contemporary Understandings of Title IX
Edited by Catherine L. Riley and Katie B. Garner

Gamification and Design Thinking in Higher Education
Case Studies for Instructional Innovation in the Economics Classroom
Carmen Bueno Muñoz, Núria Hernández Nanclares, Luis R. Murillo Zamorano, and José Ángel López Sánchez

For more information about this series, please visit: www.routledge.com/Routledge-Research-in-Higher-Education/book-series/RRHE

Gamification and Design Thinking in Higher Education
Case Studies for Instructional Innovation in the Economics Classroom

Carmen Bueno Muñoz,
Núria Hernández Nanclares,
Luis R. Murillo Zamorano
and José Ángel López Sánchez

First published 2024
by Routledge
605 Third Avenue, New York, NY 10158

and by Routledge
4 Park Square, Milton Park, Abingdon, Oxon, OX14 4RN

Routledge is an imprint of the Taylor & Francis Group, an informa business

© 2024 Carmen Bueno Muñoz, Núria Hernández Nanclares, Luis R. Murillo Zamorano, and José Ángel López Sánchez

The right of Carmen Bueno Muñoz, Núria Hernández Nanclares, Luis R. Murillo Zamorano, and José Ángel López Sánchez to be identified as authors of this work has been asserted in accordance with sections 77 and 78 of the Copyright, Designs and Patents Act 1988.

All rights reserved. No part of this book may be reprinted or reproduced or utilised in any form or by any electronic, mechanical, or other means, now known or hereafter invented, including photocopying and recording, or in any information storage or retrieval system, without permission in writing from the publishers.

Trademark notice: Product or corporate names may be trademarks or registered trademarks, and are used only for identification and explanation without intent to infringe.

ISBN: 978-1-032-66072-1 (hbk)
ISBN: 978-1-032-67541-1 (pbk)
ISBN: 978-1-032-67555-8 (ebk)

DOI: 10.4324/9781032675558

Typeset in Times New Roman
by Apex CoVantage, LLC

Contents

Acknowledgments   viii

1 Introduction   1

2 Gamification in Higher Education   6

  2.1 Introduction 6
    2.1.1 Definition 6
  2.2 Motivational and Educational Theories 8
  2.3 How to Gamify 10
    2.3.1 Analysis 10
      2.3.1.1 Analysis of Future Participants 12
    2.3.2 Design and Development 15
      2.3.2.1 Elements 16
      2.3.2.2 Duration 22
      2.3.2.3 Platforms 23
    2.3.3 Implementation and Evaluation 25
  2.4 Gamification and Other Methodologies 26
    2.4.1 Flipped Classroom 26
    2.4.2 Project-Based Learning 27

3 Design Thinking in Higher Education   37

  3.1 Introduction 37
    3.1.1 What Is Design Thinking? 38
    3.1.2 History of Design Thinking 39
    3.1.3 Models of Design Thinking 39
  3.2 Design Thinking in Higher Education 41
    3.2.1 What Students Should Learn for the 21st Century 41

3.2.2 Why Design Thinking in Higher Education 42
3.3 How to Plan a Design Thinking Process in Higher Education 43
   3.3.1 Before Beginning 43
   3.3.2 Planning to Teach Using Design Thinking 45
   3.3.3 A Road Map of the Design Thinking Process 46
   3.3.4 Examples of Design Thinking in Higher Education 47
      3.3.4.1 Example 1: "What Can This International Organization Do for You?" 47
      3.3.4.2 Example 2: "Our School Would Be Much Better If..." 51
3.4 Higher Education, COVID-19, and Design Thinking 52
   3.4.1 Remote Learning 53
   3.4.2 Equity in Education 54
   3.4.3 Community Building 54
   3.4.4 Design Thinking as a Tool for the Future 55

4 Gamification and Design Thinking Applications in Higher Education   **62**

4.1 Introduction 62
4.2 Gamification and Design Thinking in the Literature 62
4.3 How to Gamify an Activity Based on Design Thinking in Higher Education 63
4.4 Examples 66
   4.4.1 Example 1: "What Can This International Organization Do for You?" 66
      4.4.1.1 Analysis 66
      4.4.1.2 Design and Development 66
      4.4.1.3 Implementation and Evaluation 68
   4.4.2 Example 2: "Our School Would Be Much Better If..." 71
      4.4.2.1 Analysis 71
      4.4.2.2 Design and Development 71
      4.4.2.3 Implementation and Evaluation 73

5	**Ethical Issues in Gamification and Design Thinking in Higher Education**	77
	5.1 Introduction 77	
	5.2 Ethics and Higher Education 77	
	5.3 Ethics and Gamification 81	
	5.4 Ethics and Design Thinking 86	
6	**Conclusion and Final Reflections**	95
	Index	*101*

Acknowledgments

Project co-financed by the European Regional Development Fund (80%) and the Regional Government of Extremadura (file GR21009).

Proyecto cofinanciado por el Fondo Europeo de Desarrollo Regional (80%) y la Junta de Extremadura (expediente GR21009).

1 Introduction

We are in an era in which it is of vital importance in higher education to develop students' creativity and be able to offer innovative solutions in problem-solving in a context where aspects such as, for example, artificial intelligence, big data, and biotechnology, among others, are becoming increasingly important (Fadel et al., 2015; Robinson, 2016; Center for Curriculum Redesign, 2022; Zirar et al., 2023). In this sense, the World Economic Forum (2020) proposes problem-solving and creativity among its top five skills in demand for 2025.

For its part, the European Centre for the Development of Vocational Training (www.cedefop.europa.eu/en), while analyzing the skills in the online job advertisements in UE27 in 2021, identified that the five most requested are working with others (31.0%); accessing and analyzing digital data (23.0%); using digital tools for collaboration, content creation, and problem-solving (16.4%); solving problems (14.0%); and providing information and support to people (14.0%) (Cedefop, 2022). There is another series of documents along the same lines, such as "A New Skills Agenda for Europe," "Education and Training 2020" (Council of the European Union, 2009), and "Key Competences for Lifelong Learning" (European Commission, 2018, 2022) in which teamwork, creative and critical thinking, problem-solving, entrepreneurship, innovation initiative, cultural awareness, and communications are highlighted.

In this context, gamification and design thinking are powerful tools that, if used together, can enhance skills such as creativity, critical thinking and problem-solving, and collaboration (Leonard et al., 2016; Tschepe, 2018; Luka, 2019; Klock et al., 2020; Mann, 2020; Bouchrika et al., 2021; Zahedi et al., 2021; Hews et al., 2023).

Gamification is usually understood as a technique based on the use of game elements in non-ludic contexts to motivate certain behaviors of individuals (Deterding et al., 2011; Kim & Castelli, 2021; Murillo-Zamorano et al., 2021). At present, this technique is used in many sectors, the most important of which is education (Klock et al., 2020). In higher education, gamification is often used to motivate and engage students with the ultimate goal of achieving a change in their behavior (Zainuddin et al., 2020; Bouchrika et al.,

DOI: 10.4324/9781032675558-1

2021; Murillo-Zamorano et al., 2023; Huesca et al., 2023). This change in behavior can refer to an improvement in their learning outcomes (Sailer & Homner, 2020) or academic performance (Zahedi et al., 2021), among other possibilities.

Design thinking can be recognized as a human-centered approach aimed at solving challenges through innovative ways (Scheer et al., 2012; Leonard et al., 2016; Guaman-Quintanilla et al., 2018; Luka, 2019; Mann, 2020). By putting the focus on users and solutions rather than on the problem itself, design thinking engages with the people behind the problem and builds empathy with stakeholders, not losing sight of the need to offer a defined process for innovation: a step-by-step procedure that delivers meaningful and impactful solutions (Verganti, 2009; World Design Summit, 2017; Han, 2022; Magistretti et al., 2023).

This book presents an eminently practical guide for the reader interested in the fundamentals and usefulness of design thinking in contemporary higher education (Leonard et al., 2016; Mann, 2020; Han, 2022). Supported by the most relevant scientific literature and the most important design thinking models worldwide (Kolodner & Wills, 1996; Razzouk & Shute, 2012; Latorre-Cosculluela et al., 2020), we develop two original practical applications ready to be replicated by any stakeholder related to higher education. Following a truly cross-disciplinary approach, the examples presented in this book have been designed in such a way that they can be extrapolated and used in any academic discipline.

The ultimate aim of this piece of work is to analyze the joint use of gamification and design thinking in higher education. In this respect, it is worth noting that there are no experiences or practical examples of the joint use of gamification and design thinking in higher education in the current literature. In order to shed light on this domain, this book provides not one, but two concrete practical examples developed step by step, of such joint use. Both examples apply to alternative university settings, including activities carried out both inside and outside the classroom (Bowen, 2012; Fink, 2013; Murillo-Zamorano et al., 2019; Huang et al., 2023).

The joint use of gamification and design thinking carried out in this work can be easily and directly extrapolated to any other institutional context related to higher education (Villegas et al., 2019; Kessing & Löwer, 2021). These two examples could serve as a "how to" set of instructions or at least a heuristic, for the reader, to understand better the usefulness of joint use of gamification and design thinking in higher education, allowing the reader to use a similar process for their own interest. We also go a step further on the benefits of gamification and design thinking in higher education by presenting some of the most relevant questions related to various ethical issues (García-Peñalvo, 2021; Carlgren & BenMahmoud-Jouini, 2022).

This book is organized around six chapters. From this introduction, Chapter 2 analyzes gamification, defining it a priori and then going on to identify the main motivational and educational theories on which it is based, and also proposing how to gamify an activity in higher education. Chapter 3 examines design thinking, explaining what is meant by the concept, its roots, and the most important models developed to date. This is followed by a justification of how design thinking can be useful in higher education and how a design thinking process could be planned in this context. Chapter 4 is devoted to the combined study of gamification and design thinking, examining how to combine both techniques and how they can be applied to higher education. To this end, two examples in the field of higher education that simultaneously use gamification and design thinking are presented in a practical and cross-disciplinary way. Chapter 5 focuses on the most relevant ethical aspects related to gamification and design thinking in higher education identified to date. Finally, Chapter 6 proposes the conclusion and final reflections of this work.

References

Bouchrika, I., Harrati, N., Wanick, V., & Wills, G. (2021). Exploring the impact of gamification on student engagement and involvement with e-learning systems. *Interactive Learning Environments*, *29*(8), 1244–1257.

Bowen, J. A. (2012). *Teaching naked: How moving technology out of your college classroom will improve student learning*. San Francisco, CA: John Wiley & Sons.

Carlgren, L., & BenMahmoud-Jouini, S. (2022). When cultures collide: What can we learn from frictions in the implementation of design thinking? *Journal of Product Innovation Management*, *39*(1), 44–65.

Cedefop. (2022). Skills in online job advertisements. *Cedefop*. Retrieved from www.cedefop.europa.eu/en/tools/skills-intelligence/skills-online-job-advertisements?year=2021&occupation=&country=EU27_2020#1

Center for Curriculum Redesign. (2022). Retrieved from https://curriculumredesign.org/

Council of the European Union (2009). Council conclusions of 12 May 2009 on a strategic framework for European cooperation in education and training ('ET 2020'). *Official Journal of the European Union*, C 119/2, 28.5.2009.

Deterding, S., Dixon, D., Khaled, R., & Nacke, L. (2011, September). From game design elements to gamefulness: Defining gamification. In *Proceedings of the 15th international academic MindTrek conference: Envisioning future media environments* (pp. 9–15). ACM.

European Commission. (2018). Commission staff working document accompanying the document Proposal for a Council Recommendation on Key Competences for Lifelong Learning. COM (2018) 24 final, Brussels, January 17. Retrieved from https://eur-lex.europa.eu/legal-content/EN/TXT/PDF/?uri=CELEX:52018SC0014&from=EN

European Commission. (2022). Commission staff working document accompanying the document Proposal for a Council Recommendation on Key Competences for Lifelong Learning. COM (2018) 24 final, Brussels, January 17. Retrieved from https://eur-lex.europa.eu/legal-content/EN/TXT/PDF/?uri=CELEX:52018SC0014&from=EN

Fadel, C., Bialick, M., & Trilling, B. (2015). *Four-dimensional education: The competencies learners need to succeed*. Boston, MA: Center for Curriculum Redesign.

4 Introduction

Fink, L. D. (2013). *Creating significant learning experiences: An integrated approach to designing college courses*. San Francisco, CA: John Wiley & Sons.

García-Peñalvo, F. J. (2021). Avoiding the dark side of digital transformation in teaching. An institutional reference framework for eLearning in higher education. *Sustainability*, *13*(4), 2023.

Guaman-Quintanilla, S., Chiluiza, K., Everaert, P., & Valcke, M. (2018). Design thinking in higher education: A scoping review. In *11th annual international conference of education, research and innovation (ICERI)* (pp. 2954–2963). International Academy of Technology, Education and Development (IATED).

Han, E. (2022). What is design thinking & why is it important? *HBS Online*. Retrieved from https://online.hbs.edu/blog/post/what-is-design-thinking

Hews, R., Beligatamulla, G., & McNamara, J. (2023). Creative confidence and thinking skills for lawyers: Making sense of design thinking pedagogy in legal education. *Thinking Skills and Creativity*, *49*, 101352.

Huang, A. Y., Lu, O. H., & Yang, S. J. (2023). Effects of artificial intelligence–enabled personalized recommendations on learners' learning engagement, motivation, and outcomes in a flipped classroom. *Computers & Education*, *194*, 104684.

Huesca, G., Campos, G., Larre, M., & Pérez-Lezama, C. (2023). Implementation of a mixed strategy of gamification and flipped learning in undergraduate basic programming courses. *Education Sciences*, *13*(5), 474.

Kessing, D., & Löwer, M. (2020, October). Work-in-progress: Gamification and design thinking–A motivational analysis of an international, interdisciplinary, team-based university course. In *International conference on interactive collaborative and blended learning* (pp. 65–73). Cham: Springer.

Kim, J., & Castelli, D. M. (2021). Effects of gamification on behavioral change in education: A meta-analysis. *International Journal of Environmental Research and Public Health*, *18*(7), 3550.

Klock, A. C. T., Gasparini, I., Pimenta, M. S., & Hamari, J. (2020). Tailored gamification: A review of literature. *International Journal of Human-Computer Studies*, *144*, 102495.

Kolodner, J. L., & Wills, L. M. (1996). Powers of observation in creative design. *Design Studies*, *17*(4), 385–416.

Latorre-Cosculluela, C., Vázquez-Toledo, S., Rodríguez-Martínez, A., & Liesa-Orús, M. (2020). Design thinking: Creatividad y pensamiento crítico en la universidad. *Revista Electrónica de Investigación Educativa*, *22*. https://doi.org/10.24320/redie.2020.22.e28.2917

Leonard, S. N., Fitzgerald, R. N., & Riordan, G. (2016). Using developmental evaluation as a design thinking tool for curriculum innovation in professional higher education. *Higher Education Research & Development*, *35*(2), 309–321.

Luka, I. (2019). Design thinking in pedagogy: Frameworks and uses. *European Journal of Education*, *54*(4), 499–512. https://doi.org/10.1111/ejed.12367

Magistretti, S., Dell'Era, C., Cautela, C., & Kotlar, J. (2023). Design thinking for organizational innovation at PepsiCo. *California Management Review*, *65*(3), 5–26.

Mann, C. (2020). Advising by design: Co-creating advising services with students for their success. *Frontiers in Education*, *5*, 9. https://doi.org/10.3389/feduc.2020.00099

Murillo-Zamorano, L. R., López-Sánchez, J. A., & Godoy-Caballero, A. L. (2019). How the flipped classroom affects knowledge, skills, and engagement in higher education: Effects on students' satisfaction. *Computers & Education*, *141*, 103608.

Murillo-Zamorano, L. R., López-Sánchez, J. Á., Godoy-Caballero, A. L., & Bueno-Muñoz, C. (2021). Gamification and active learning in higher education: Is it possible to match digital society, academia and students' interests? *International Journal of Educational Technology in Higher Education, 18*, 15.

Murillo-Zamorano, L. R., López-Sánchez, J. A., López-Rey, M. J., & Bueno-Muñoz, C. (2023). Gamification in higher education: The ECOn+ star battles. *Computers & Education, 194*, 104699.

Razzouk, R., & Shute, V. (2012). What is design thinking and why is it important? *Review of Educational Research, 82*(3), 330–348.

Robinson, K. (2016). Do schools kill creativity? *TED Talk*. Retrieved from www.ted.com/talks/sir_ken_robinson_do_schools_kill_creativity?language=es

Sailer, M., & Homner, L. (2020). The gamification of learning: A meta-analysis. *Educational Psychology Review, 32*, 77–112.

Scheer, A., Noweski, C., & Meinel, C. (2012). Transforming constructivist learning into action: Design thinking in education. *Design and Technology Education: An International Journal, 17*(3).

Tschepe, S. (2018). How design thinking can benefit education. *The Startup | Medium*. Retrieved from https://medium.com/swlh/how-design-thinking-can-benefit-education-2bba35450771

Verganti, R. (2009). *Design driven innovation: Changing the rules of competition by radically innovating what things mean*. Boston, Massachusetts: Harvard Business Press.

Villegas, E., Labrador, E., Fonseca, D., Fernández-Guinea, S., & Moreira, F. (2019, July). Design thinking and gamification: User centered methodologies. In *International conference on human-computer interaction* (pp. 115–124). Cham: Springer.

World Design Summit. (2017). *Montreal design declaration 2017*. Retrieved from www.designdeclaration.org/wp-content/uploads/2019/01/Montreal_Design_Declaration_2017_WEB.pdf

World Economic Forum. (2020). *The future of jobs report 2020*. Retrieved from https://www.weforum.org/reports/the-future-of-jobs-report-2020/in-full/infographics-e4e69e4de7

Zahedi, L., Batten, J., Ross, M., Potvin, G., Damas, S., Clarke, P., & Davis, D. (2021). Gamification in education: A mixed-methods study of gender on computer science students' academic performance and identity development. *Journal of Computing in Higher Education, 33*(2), 441–474.

Zainuddin, Z., Chu, S. K. W., Shujahat, M., & Perera, C. J. (2020). The impact of gamification on learning and instruction: A systematic review of empirical evidence. *Educational Research Review, 30*, 100326.

Zirar, A., Ali, S. I., & Islam, N. (2023). Worker and workplace Artificial Intelligence (AI) coexistence: Emerging themes and research agenda. *Technovation, 124*, 102747.

2 Gamification in Higher Education

2.1 Introduction

Gamification is a design technique based on the use of game elements in other contexts to motivate and encourage certain behaviors on the part of individuals (Deterding et al., 2011; Kim & Castelli, 2021; Murillo-Zamorano et al., 2021). At present, this technique is used in many sectors, the most important of which is education (Klock et al., 2020).

In higher education, gamification is often used to motivate and engage students (Bouchrika et al., 2021; Murillo-Zamorano et al., 2023). Studies show that gamification has a positive effect on students and that motivation is a predictor of academic achievement (Zainuddin et al., 2020). The ultimate goal of gamification is to achieve a change in user behavior. In the context of higher education, this change in behavior can refer to an improvement in their learning outcomes (Sailer & Homner, 2020) or academic performance (Zahedi et al., 2021), among other possibilities.

In this chapter, we examine gamification. To accomplish this goal, we first delimit its definition. Subsequently, we study the main motivational and educational theories on which the studies in this context are based. Thereafter, we explain how to gamify an activity in higher education. In this section, we discuss in detail the steps that constitute the gamification process. Finally, we address the combination of gamification with certain educational methodologies.

2.1.1 Definition

The concept of gamification emerged in 2008 and began to attract interest in 2010 (Deterding et al., 2011, Dehghanzadeh et al., 2023). Numerous authors have proposed various definitions of the term *gamification* since this concept is subject to study. However, at present, no consensus has been reached regarding what gamification is (Bagheri et al., 2020; Staller & Koerner, 2021).

Faust (2021) divides definitions of gamification into two categories depending on the perspective they take: definitions from a structural point of view and definitions from an interactive point of view. From a structural point of view, gamification is defined on the basis of the structure of the task or system that is gamified. Gamification is incorporated into these tasks or systems to act as an incentive due to its ludic quality. This category includes definitions that follow the definition proposed by Deterding et al. (2011, p. 10): "the use of game design elements in non-game contexts."

However, in recent years, some authors have adopted a new approach that advocates the creation of user-centered experiences. From an interactive point of view, "gamification results from a human-task interaction, and therefore also depends on individual perception" (Faust, 2021, p. 9). This approach stems from the definition proposed by Huotari and Hamari (2017, p. 25), who state that gamification is "a process of enhancing a service with affordances for gameful experiences in order to support user's overall value creation."

According to this approach, a gamified experience arises from a process of cocreation between the activity itself and its users, leading to an experience that is similar to those associated with games (Tanouri et al., 2022). That is, from a structural point of view, a gamified activity is taken into account in terms of the game elements that are integrated within it. From an interactive point of view, on the other hand, the experience cannot be understood without the participation of the user who, through his actions, gives rise to a process of cocreation by providing value (Wolf et al., 2020). In summary, we can say that gamification uses game elements to create motivating experiences and that these experiences take place through interactions among the participants.

So far, we have differentiated two approaches that can be taken to gamification definitions: definitions from a structural point of view and definitions from an interactive point of view, as proposed by Faust (2021). However, these are only some of the classifications found in the literature. Khaldi et al. (2023), based on Saggah et al. (2020), differentiate three approaches according to the level of detail with which they approach their study in the educational environment: high-level approach, gamification elements guidance approach, and scenario-based approach. The high-level approach encompasses those works that approach gamification from a broad perspective without determining characteristics such as the elements used and the implementation process. Under the gamification elements guidance approach, it is pointed out which elements to use, and, generally, a guide to applying the gamified design is offered. Finally, the scenario-based approach refers to those empirical studies in which the design process that has been carried out is described.

In addition to delimiting the concept of gamification, it is interesting to examine the differences between games and gamified experiences. Some authors have claimed that it is necessary to make such a distinction to determine when a gamified activity is being implemented and when a game is simply being used for educational purposes. For example, Fontana (2020) claims to employ gamification to teach chemistry during the COVID-19 pandemic and subsequently refers to the same activity as the use of a serious game in this context. A serious game is a game whose purpose is not to entertain but rather to teach or inform (Alvarez & Djaouti, 2011). Serious games are also called games for a purpose, productivity games, and behavioral games, among other terms (Baptista & Oliveira, 2019). These differences between games and gamification must be clarified. Duggal et al. (2021) identify several such differences, including the following. Regarding objectives, games have short-term objectives, while gamification has long-term objectives. Regarding their motivation, games are intended to teach a specific skill, while gamification is intended to complement the pedagogical system in use. Finally, games exhibit a structure based on play and training, while gamification focuses on influencing user motivation and engagement.

It should also be noted that we find a division of opinions about the relationship between gamification and technology. Some authors, such as Bizzi (2023), state that gamification is based on the use of technology. More precisely, he defines it within organizations as "the use of information technology (IT) for the application of features, elements, and techniques typical of games in the work context to influence the way in which employees perform tasks" (Bizzi, 2023, p. 1). Other authors, such as Wei et al. (2023), argue that, although the use of digital technology often supports gamification, it is not a prerequisite. This point is related to the above since gamification is sometimes confused with digital games (Wei et al., 2023).

After defining the concept of gamification and differentiating it from the concept of serious games, in the following section, we explain the theories on which gamification studies are based.

2.2 Motivational and Educational Theories

Studies that address gamification and its effects are usually based on a variety of theories to support their findings. According to the recent review conducted by Krath et al. (2021), the main theories on which research on gamification is based are Deci and Ryan's self-determination theory (1985, 2000) and Csíkszentmihályi's flow theory (1975, 1990). Both theories focus on aspects related to the motivation of individuals.

Specifically, self-determination theory (Deci & Ryan, 1985, 2000) differentiates between extrinsic motivation and intrinsic motivation. The former type of motivation originates outside the individual, who performs a given action due to being motivated by the reward that he or she is to obtain in return. Intrinsic motivation, conversely, comes from within. In this case, the individual engages in an activity due to its own characteristics because he or she considers it to be interesting or entertaining. Csíkszentmihályi's flow theory (1975, 1990) focuses on the state of flow. In this state, the individual is immersed in and totally focused on what he or she is doing at that moment. The task is an end in itself, not a result. During the flow state, the individual's perception of time is distorted, and his or her self-consciousness disappears.

These two theories, self-determination theory and flow theory, are based on the study of motivation. The goal of gamification is to influence the motivation of individuals and thereby achieve a change in their behavior (Koivisto & Hamari, 2019). Therefore, it seems reasonable to maintain that these two theories are the most predominant in research addressing the topic of gamification. As mentioned in the introduction to this chapter, gamification is a technique that is used in a variety of disparate contexts.

At present, we find examples of gamified activities in areas such as corporate training (Wang et al., 2022), online travel agents platforms (Shi et al., 2022), recycling (Hsu, 2022), and manufacturing (Keepers et al., 2022). It is reasonable to maintain that the theories with the greatest presence in research on gamification are those that are based on motivation. However, this fact does not entail a lack of other relevant theories.

This book focuses on the use of gamification and design thinking in higher education. For this reason, it is also interesting to examine the most common learning theories in the study of gamification. A study conducted by Krath et al. (2021) identifies the following three theories as the most relevant: experiential learning theory (Kolb, 1984), constructivist learning theory (Jonassen & Rohrer-Murphy, 1999; Piaget, 1977), and cognitive load theory, that was proposed by Sweller (1988). Most studies regarding gamification are based on these three learning theories.

According to Kolbs' experiential learning theory (1984), knowledge is acquired through experience. More precisely, learning refers to the process that learners must use to adapt to and cope with problems, receive feedback, and obtain knowledge through an iterative learning cycle. Constructivist learning theory (Jonassen & Rohrer-Murphy, 1999; Piaget, 1977) claims that knowledge is constructed by learners and not merely transmitted to them. Finally, cognitive load theory (Sweller, 1988) focuses on the processing capacity of learners. This theory highlights the fact that the presence of unnecessary cognitive loads distracts learners and that the minimization of such loads facilitates the processing of learning content.

Nevertheless, theories regarding motivation, especially self-determination theory, are the most frequently used in this context. Therefore, throughout this book, we focus on the extrinsic motivation and intrinsic motivation of participants in gamified experiences. In the literature, a large number of studies demonstrate the ability of gamification to influence both extrinsic motivation (e.g., Ferriz-Valero et al., 2020, Navarro et al., 2023) and intrinsic motivation (Xu et al., 2021; Kam & Umar, 2023).

However, what is most desirable when designing a gamified experience is to promote the intrinsic motivation of users (Koivisto & Hamari, 2019). This type of motivation, unlike extrinsic motivation, is linked to long-term engagement. Therefore, if we want users to participate in the experience continuously over a period of time, it is advisable to create activities that influence this type of motivation.

Following these comments on the main theories on which gamification studies are based, in the following section, we explain how an activity is gamified by distinguishing the three main steps that constitute this process.

2.3 How to Gamify

The literature contains different proposals for the process of gamification (e.g., Cechetti et al., 2019; De la Peña et al., 2021; Deterding, 2015). From these proposals, it follows that the main three steps that must be considered to develop a gamified experience are (i) analysis (Cechetti et al., 2019), (ii) design and development (De la Peña et al., 2021), and (iii) implementation and evaluation (Deterding, 2015). As for the analysis step, the literature referred to earlier focuses on the examination of the activity to be gamified and its context, the determination of objectives, and the exploration of future participants. The design and development step is defined as the study of gamification in similar activities as well as the construction of such activities by the incorporation of elements, duration, and platforms. Finally, the implementation and evaluation step concerns the application of the activity, the assessment of results, and the design modification (if necessary). More in detail, the above three steps are explained in the following subsections.

2.3.1 Analysis

The first step in the creation of a gamified activity consists of analyzing the context and characteristics of the task to be gamified itself. The main actions performed during the analysis phase are the following: examine the nature of the activity to be gamified, identify the objectives to be pursued through gamification, and study the nature of future participants in the gamification process as well as their behavior.

Examining and delimiting the characteristics of the activity to be gamified represent the first step in the creation process. Namely, the distinctive features of the environment condition the available design possibilities. Among the features that must be taken into account in this context are the number of learners involved, the degree of difficulty of the subject matter, and the duration of the activity (Sezgin & Yüzer, 2022). The available technology should also be taken into account. For example, if an activity is based on a distance learning methodology, the creation process should take into account the fact that the interaction between the teacher and the students is to take place via digital media, making the existence of sufficient technological resources necessary to ensure its proper functioning. Likewise, if the experience is to take place inside the classroom and requires the use of devices with internet connections, it must be ensured that all students have access to such a device.

The objectives of the process also condition the available design possibilities. Gamification is not merely a matter of adding game elements to an activity and assuming that these elements will motivate learners. Gamification should be used to achieve a specific goal. To create a gamified design that helps achieve this goal, the first step is to define the goal in question. As Liu et al. (2017) argue, the design must exhibit congruence; these authors give as an example the incoherence implied by the introduction of leaderboards if the aim of the activity is not to compare the achievements of the participants.

Analyzing future participants and their behavior is essential for the next phase, which consists of the design and development of the gamified activity. Both the task of defining the environment and objectives and an awareness of the nature of the future participants are necessary steps in the subsequent selection of the most appropriate gamification structure and elements that allow us to confer meaning on the activity and align its purpose with the motivations and interests of the participants (Floryan et al., 2019, 2020). Participant analysis is a broad topic that has been widely addressed in the literature. Given its depth, this topic is discussed in further detail in the following subsection.

It should be noted that a new approach has been developed that advocates the customization of the gamified experience for each user. However, as Oliveira et al. (2023) note following their review of the literature on this subject in the field of education, further research is necessary to investigate the possibilities of offering gamified experiences that are tailored to each learner as well as the effects of such possibilities.

In any case, this task of personalization becomes easier if we make use of technology. Bennani et al. (2022) review the literature on adaptive gamification in the context of e-learning. These authors conclude that the application of this approach remains limited and that it could benefit from the use of artificial intelligence to offer a more dynamic experience. These authors also note that, to facilitate future adaptive learning applications based on artificial intelligence, the system should capture and analyze data concerning the learner himself or herself (his or her skills, motivation, and learning style, among other factors) as well as data concerning the learner's interaction with the system (his or her engagement and feelings of belonging and competence, among other factors). The analysis of these factors can facilitate the creation of an experience tailored to each learner by the intelligent system.

As previously mentioned, the analysis of future participants is a relevant topic, as evidenced by the fact that such analysis has attracted attention from academia in recent years (González-González et al., 2022; Scheibe & Zimmer, 2022), particularly since the effects of gamification seem to vary according to the characteristics of its users (Denden et al., 2022). For this reason, in the following, we focus on the individuals targeted by the gamification proposed in this book. That is, we address the characteristics of current university students—Generation Z—and the various classifications of students in gamified environments.

2.3.1.1 Analysis of Future Participants

As mentioned, studying the characteristics of the individuals who are to participate in our gamified experience is essential, since the results we obtain depend to a greater or lesser extent on these characteristics. Studies show that various elements of gamification may not affect individuals in the same ways depending on their traits. Denden et al. (2022) conducted a meta-analysis to investigate this topic in the field of education and concluded that the results of gamification depend on the characteristics of the students involved in this activity. These authors also note that the most frequently analyzed characteristic is the personality of the students and argue that more research should be conducted to deepen our knowledge in this respect.

It should be noted that uncertainty remains regarding the ways in which some individual traits affect the ability of gamification to achieve a given outcome since different studies report contradictory results. For example, according to the research conducted by Putz et al. (2020), the effects of gamification on students do not depend on students' gender or age. However, research conducted by Denden et al. (2021) and Pakinee and Puritat (2021) suggests that variables such as gender and personality do affect the impact of gamification.

Subsequently, we examine the characteristics of the participants in the gamified experiences who are the focus of this book: college students. On the one hand, we analyze the traits of Generation Z, which is the generation to which most current college students belong. Generation Z is composed of individuals who were born at the end of the 20th century and the beginning of the 21st century. It should be noted that there is no consensus regarding the year in which this generation begins. Some authors identify individuals born since 1995 as members of Generation Z; others take 1997 as the generation's; and finally, some authors consider Generation Z to include individuals born since 2000 (Szymkowiak et al., 2021). In any case, these individuals represent the current generation of university students.

On the other hand, after commenting on the characteristics of this generation, we detail some classifications of various types of students in the context of gamification. The objective of this analysis is to focus in greater depth on the nature of future participants to create gamified experiences that are capable of influencing them.

GENERATION Z

As mentioned, analyzing the characteristics of future participants in a gamified experience represents one of the first steps in the design process. The participants in gamified activities in higher education include, at present, students who belong to Generation Z. This generation, born after members of Generation Y, otherwise known as Millennials, is formed by digital natives. The intensive use of technology is a distinctive feature of this population group (Szymkowiak et al., 2021). Therefore, it is unsurprising that studies note that this generation is more prone to the adoption of new educational technologies than the previous generation (Kuleto et al., 2021).

The truth is that Generation Z exhibits different educational preferences. Recent generations of university students use electronic devices, primarily their smartphones, both inside and outside the classroom, and they introduce these devices into the learning process by searching for information using the internet and explanatory videos (Yastibas et al., 2021). Other educational methods for which they exhibit a preference are interactive games and virtual learning environments (Vizcaya-Moreno & Pérez-Cañaveras, 2020; Wijayaratna et al., 2023). Therefore, one characteristic that should be borne in mind when designing a gamified activity aimed at Generation Z is the possibility of introducing the use of digital technology to attract their interest in the activity.

Another characteristic that sets members of Generation Z apart is their individualism. Pichler et al. (2021) highlight the problem that the individualism that characterizes Generation Z poses for companies. Currently, companies demand professionals who are able to work on teams. However, recent generations of students, that is, those who will enter the job market in the coming years, prefer to work in isolation. For this reason, it is essential to promote the importance of teams and collaboration among colleagues. This competence in teamwork can be promoted by the use of gamified designs that include elements that facilitate social interaction and cooperation among learners.

TYPES OF LEARNERS VERSUS GAMIFICATION

In addition to maintaining a focus on the characteristics of the future participants in the gamified activity to be developed, it is advisable to be aware of the various types of users that exist in the context of gamification. Namely, the ability to influence variables such as motivation in an educational environment depends on the type of user of the gamified activity represented by each student (Bovermann & Bastiaens, 2020).

The most frequent classification of gamers in the relevant literature is that proposed by Bartle (1996). This classification originally referred to users of online multiplayer video games but is currently applied to all types of games as well as to gamified experiences (e.g., Ayastuy et al., 2021; Sakharova et al., 2023). Bartle (1996) differentiates among four types of players according to their main objective when participating in the game: (i) achievers—whose goal is to accumulate the highest number of achievements; (ii) explorers—who seek to discover and explore the platform on which the experience takes place; (iii) socializers—who seek to establish relationships with other players; and (iv) killers—whose goal is to win the game and eliminate the rest of the players.

In the field of education, various authors have recently proposed different classifications. Dichev et al. (2020) distinguish among five types of students in accordance with their motivation (intrinsic, extrinsic, or none) and their perception of their own degree of ability (high or low). The five types of learners in the context of gamification identified by Dichev et al. (2020) are defined next:

- Capable explorer: these learners believe in themselves and find learning to be interesting. They seek to solve problems and develop their own skills and competencies. Difficult tasks are an attractive challenge for them.
- Struggling explorer: these learners strive to learn and, like capable explorers, want to improve their skills. However, they have less confidence in their skills. They avoid a task if they perceive it to be unachievable in an attempt to prevent the emergence of a feeling of disappointment if they fail to achieve their goal.
- Capable benefit seeker: these learners are not interested in the educational activity itself but rather in the reward they can obtain by engaging in the activity. Such a reward may consist, for example, of good grades or the admiration of peers. These learners are self-confident and consider themselves to be skilled.
- Struggling benefit seeker: these learners students are not very responsible and seek to pass the class but are not enthusiastic about acquiring and improving their knowledge and skills. They devote little effort to their studies and avoid tasks that they consider to be difficult.
- Indifferent: these students are not motivated to participate in gamified educational activities. The origin of their lack of motivation can be found both in their lack of skills and in the perceived low value of the gamified experience.

The classification proposed by Dichev et al. (2020) just discussed is based on motivation and perceived learner abilities as a foundation for the various categories. However, these are not the only factors that can be used to classify learners in a gamified environment. For example, Cömert and Samur (2021) draw on several existing models of player types and combine them with educational theories to propose their own model, which identifies seven distinct types. The seven player types described by Cömert and Samur (2021) in the educational context are as follows:

- Entertainers: these learners participate in the experience to have fun. They enjoy the whole process and do not care about its outcome. This model considers all participants to be entertainers at the beginning of the activity since it assumes that they enter the activity for the purpose of entertainment and subsequently exhibit different behaviors.

- Strategic: the goal of these learners is to win. To accomplish this goal, they employ critical thinking and logical-mathematical intelligence.
- Leaders: these learners are dominant players who exhibit high levels of interpersonal and linguistic skills. They guide the group and participate both with the aim of winning and as a result of the excitement generated by the game.
- Researchers: these learners are curious and interested in the game environment and the associated characters. They possess intrapersonal and naturalistic intelligence.
- Testers: these learners want to discover all the options available as part of the experience and are bold and courageous. They differ from researchers in that the latter do not play with an ultimate goal in mind whereas testers aim to win.
- Artists: these learners attribute great importance to aesthetics and value visual and auditory elements. Their linguistic, spatial, and musical intelligence are noteworthy. No type of player in the models proposed by other authors resembles this type.
- Socializers: these learners participate in the experience to make friends and feel as if they are part of a group. They possess interpersonal intelligence and communicate easily with other players.

We must bear in mind the classifications thus examined when creating gamified experiences and evaluating their results. From this perspective, it is clear that each student may exhibit a different attitude or behavior toward gamification. Teachers should be aware of these differences and develop strategies that promote the motivation of students who exhibit less interest in these activities.

Finally, it should be noted that other aspects also affect the results of gamification in educational environments. According to the study conducted by Ahmad et al. (2021), the effects of gamification on different variables, such as the motivation, effort, and interest exhibited by the students, differ depending on the number of students participating in the activity.

2.3.2 Design and Development

Following the analysis phase, the designers determine the nature of the future gamified experience. In other words, the second step of the gamification process corresponds to the design and development phase of the activity. We can initiate this step by examining the designs that have been applied in similar activities as well as their results. This examination is followed by the conception and construction of the experience.

Examining previous activities can help us understand the designs that have been chosen for certain contexts and the implications that have been derived from their application (Cechetti et al., 2019). This analysis can be viewed as a source of information that can serve as a guide and an inspiration. As mentioned earlier, we must take the nature of the activity to be gamified into account, define its objectives, and bear in mind the nature of its future participants. Therefore, based on this analysis of successful gamified designs, we must develop our own experience and adapt it to the particular characteristics of its environment. In contrast, it is not advisable merely to copy gamified designs even if they have led to good results in other environments (Diefenbach & Müssig, 2019).

In summary, starting the design and development phase by examining the ways in which gamification has been used in similar environments can make it easier for us to develop our activity successfully. This subphase helps us make decisions regarding the design of the activity, thus allowing us to make better-informed decisions. In addition, knowing which previous gamified activities have not led to the expected results allows us to avoid making the same design mistakes.

After gathering information concerning the environment, objectives, participants, and previous gamified designs, we proceed to determine the nature of our gamified experience and construct it. To accomplish this goal, the necessary materials, such as slides, texts, and videos, are developed, as is the design of various gamification elements, such as badges and other rewards. In the ideation or conception phase of the activity, the features of the experience are delimited, which conditions its future development. The possibilities of gamification design are extensive, and the task of exploring the various characteristics that a gamified design can have as well as the existing alternatives for developing such a design is of great interest.

For all these reasons, as in the case of the previous point concerning the analysis of the participants, we explore this topic in further detail next. Specifically, we focus on the conception of the activity, its characteristics, identifying the elements of gamification that are present, its duration and the possible use of platforms in this context. We then investigate these features, explaining various alternatives and facilitating decision-making regarding the design of the activity.

2.3.2.1 Elements

The most widespread definition of gamification is offered by Deterding et al. (2011), which states that gamification is related to the application of game elements in contexts other than games. However, what are these game elements? Academics have attempted to answer this question over the past two decades. Numerous authors have proposed different classifications and taxonomies of the elements that can be integrated into a gamified design. Two of the most widely used such classifications in the relevant literature are those offered by Werbach and Hunter (2012) and Hunicke et al. (2004).

On the one hand, Werbach and Hunter (2012) distinguish among three categories of gamification elements: dynamics, mechanics, and components. Hunicke et al. (2004), on the other hand, propose the mechanics, dynamics, and aesthetic (MDA) framework. Although the MDA framework is commonly used in the study of gamification, its origins lie in the field of game design. Therefore, Robson et al. (2015) adapt this framework to gamification to develop the MDE (mechanics, dynamics, and emotions) framework.

There are notable differences between these proposals and those of other researchers. According to Schöbel et al. (2020), some taxonomies are incomplete because they do not include certain elements, while others include several elements under a single category.

The truth is that no final list of elements has yet been developed, but their use is subject to the decisions of the designers of these experiences. The taxonomy proposed by Toda et al. (2019) focuses on gamification in educational environments. The taxonomy developed by Toda et al. (2019) comprises five dimensions: performance/measurement, ecological, social, personal, and fictional. In the following, we discuss the main features of these categories as well as the elements they include.

PERFORMANCE/MEASUREMENT ELEMENTS

The elements included in the performance/measurement category are used to provide feedback to learners and guide them regarding their performance of the activities. This category focuses on the response of the environment to the user's actions. The elements included in this category are points, badges, levels, progress, and stats. Points are the most commonly used gamification element in different contexts (Ekici, 2021; Mavroeidi et al., 2019) and are present in most gamified processes. This fact may be because points serve as a foundation for other elements (Albertazzi et al., 2019). For example, badges, which are visual representations of achievements, can be awarded if a certain number of points are accumulated. Another example of this category is levels. The designer of the gamified experience can stipulate that a necessary condition for a participant to access subsequent levels or stages is to accumulate a certain number of points.

In any case, levels form part of this category (performance/measurement) if the activity stipulates that a user must achieve a performance-related objective to advance to higher levels. In such a situation, we can say that levels are indicative of the user's progress in the activity (van der Lubbe et al., 2021). Although Toda et al. (2019) do not mention this point, levels would not indicate progress or offer feedback to learners regarding their performance if access to subsequent levels is allowed as a function of events that are not connected to the user. For example, in a gamified activity aimed at college students, levels indicate learners' progress if they must complete the previous level successfully to gain access. However, if they are allowed to participate in new levels based on the date, the levels would belong to another category of elements. Specifically, in this case, levels would resemble the novelty element, which is included in the personal category.

ECOLOGICAL ELEMENTS

The next category of gamification elements described by Toda et al. (2019) is ecological. This category refers to the environment in which gamification is implemented. The ecological category is formed by the elements of chance, imposed choice, economy, rarity, and time pressure. To our knowledge, the use of the first three elements—chance, imposed choice, and economy—is not very widespread, and there are hardly any references to these elements in the relevant literature. One such study is conducted by Zecri et al. (2021), who include imposed choices in their analysis of the elements of gamification in educational applications.

The rarity element refers to limited or scarce items or resources. Milanesi et al. (2022) study the inclusion of rarity in a gamified mobile application developed for the luxury industry. This mobile application includes rare items that are collectible and generate points for users if they manage to obtain them. In this context, the rarity of the items generates a feeling of exclusivity, which is closely linked to the luxury industry and can influence the motivation of the participants. Focusing on the field of higher education, Jodoi et al. (2021) include the element of rarity in an educational app via the creation of limited resources. According to these authors, the objective of the inclusion of this element is to generate engagement among university students.

Finally, the most prominent element in this category is time pressure. Anunpattana et al. (2021) note that the time available must be adjusted to make it feasible for students to achieve the objectives of the activity. Otherwise, students will be unable to complete the task. Anunpattana et al. (2021) conduct an experiment to analyze the effects of this element on learners and conclude that it promotes their engagement and motivation. Finally, time pressure can be introduced in different ways in the context of a gamified activity depending on the characteristics of the activity itself. For example, we can set a deadline to complete a task. If we have the necessary devices, we can display a countdown or a clock visually on screens.

SOCIAL ELEMENTS

Another category of gamification elements noted by Toda et al. (2019) is the social category. Social elements refer to those that allow interaction between learners. Toda et al. (2019) identify the following: competition (or leaderboards), cooperation (or teams), reputation, and social pressure. In this context, it should be noted that leaderboards promote competition among students by allowing them to compare their merits, which are arranged in a table and displayed visually. These leaderboards are updated periodically, which allows participants to increase their position if their performance increases. The objective of this comparison of results is to motivate students to continue making efforts to complete the activity by allowing them to obtain satisfaction from the recognition of the rest of the group if they reach the top of the leaderboard (Da Silva Júnior et al., 2022; Na & Han, 2023).

However, although Toda et al. (2019) link competition with leaderboards, a link which is widely accepted in the literature, insufficient studies have been conducted to ensure that other elements are not equally or more effective in promoting comparisons among users. As van Gaalen et al. (2021) note, it is possible that other, less competitive elements, such as upgrading avatars and badges, also promote comparisons among participants. In other words, these elements could also be considered social elements.

When designing a gamified experience, we may wonder whether we should opt for an activity in which students compete or, on the contrary, whether we should opt for a cooperative experience in which students collaborate with each other. According to the meta-analysis conducted by Sailer and Homner (2020), the effects of gamification on learning outcomes, both motivational and behavioral, depend on the type of social interaction that is involved in the gamified activities. These authors conclude that the effects of gamification in an environment in which collaboration and competition among students are combined are greater than in environments in which students only compete. Likewise, we must be cautious when establishing the terms of competition. Putting excessive pressure on participants in a competitive environment can decrease their intrinsic motivation (Featherstone & Habgood, 2019).

Other elements that are also included in this category, although they are not noted by Toda et al. (2019), include chats and forums. Chats and forums allow communication between participants when the experience takes place remotely. These functions can be included in the gamified platform used for the activity or, on the contrary, an external platform can be used for this purpose. For example, Díaz-Ramírez (2020) uses the instant messaging application WhatsApp to allow students to communicate in the gamified educational experience he developed. His study reveals that this element is widely accepted by participants. On the forums, students can read and respond to posts from their peers and create their own posts (Denden et al., 2019; Zhu et al., 2023).

Gamification, although it can be implemented without resorting to new technologies, is a phenomenon that is closely linked to digitalization (Pasca et al., 2021; Sadovets et al., 2022). In recent decades, we have witnessed unstoppable growth in the use of social networks (Laor, 2022). Some designers of gamified experiences have highlighted the potential of social networks to act as a motivational element by appealing to individuals on the social level.

As mentioned, reputation and social pressure are linked to the interactions among users. Reputation and social pressure linked to gamification are limited to the community formed by the participants in the gamified experience. If we introduce social networks into the experience and allow users to share their achievements via these networks (Vanolo, 2018; Yang & Li, 2021), the community of individuals to which they are exposed becomes larger. For example, we can allow participants to share the badges the earn while participating in an experience via their social networks. Sharing badges is motivating for individuals (Sheffler et al., 2020; Cheng et al., 2023). In this way, we could increase users' motivation by allowing them to receive recognition from a larger number of people.

PERSONAL ELEMENTS

Personal elements pertain to the learner who participates in the gamified experience. This category includes missions, challenges, novelty, renovation, and visual and auditory sensations.

Missions are short tasks associated with a specific objective. Tenório et al. (2022) propose employing missions to adapt the gamified design during the experience to attract the attention of certain participants. Specifically, these argue that teachers can use missions to motivate and increase the level of participation of students who exhibit lower performance. To accomplish this task, the teacher should monitor the way in which each of the students behaves and determine whether the level of participation exhibited by any student is lower than expected. In addition, missions can be linked with the ability to obtain other elements, such as points, badges, and levels.

Challenges, like missions, are tasks associated with a defined objective. The difference between these two elements lies in the fact that, in addition, the level of difficulty of a challenge increases as the gamified activity progresses (Barata et al., 2017). This increase in difficulty allows challenges to be used as a form of training for more complex activities in the future while maintaining the motivation of the participants (Yen et al., 2019; Ramos Aguiar et al., 2023). It should be noted that some authors use the term *challenge* to refer both to what we have defined as challenges and to missions and tasks (e.g., Koivisto and Hamari (2019).

Novelty refers to the generation of a feeling of surprise in the participants. Renovation refers to the ability, drawn from games, to increase the number of lives available to the individual. This element can only be introduced if the design of our experience stipulates that participants have a certain number of lives and notes that they can lose those lives if they commit certain actions. Finally, the visual and auditory sensations provided by a gamified experience have an effect on individuals. For example, Harman and Brown (2022) introduce visual sensations through the use of illustrations. However, according to their study, these stimuli do not generate any reactions in participants.

FICTIONAL ELEMENTS

Finally, the elements included in the fictional category are those that give meaning to the experience. Toda et al. (2019) include narrative and storytelling in this category. Although these terms tend to be used synonymously (e.g., Mazarakis & Bräuer, 2023; Chan & Baig, 2023), Toda et al. (2019) use the concept of narrative to refer to the order of events during the gamified experience, while they use the term *storytelling* to refer to the story or script that serves as a common thread throughout the activity.

This category is similar to what Hervás et al. (2017) call the immersion category. According to these authors, immersive elements are those that promote deep involvement in the gamified activity. This category includes, in addition to narrative, exploration, and avatars. Exploration refers to strategies that aim to encourage the user to discover all the particularities of the game. An avatar is a graphic illustration of the user within the gamified experience (Denden et al., 2021).

At present, it is common to rely on a combination of gamification elements in the experiences developed for higher education (Saxena & Mishra, 2021). These elements can be connected to each other and may resort to fictional elements to give meaning to the whole experience. For example, Rincon-Flores et al. (2022) create a gamified activity based on badges, avatars, and leaderboards. These authors design badges that are inspired by well-known superheroes. Introducing narratives that are familiar and appealing to learners can make it easier for learners to engage in the activity. Cechella et al. (2021) combine avatars, points, and progress in such a way as to ensure that each student's personalized avatar displays his or her progress bar based on his or her performance and the number of points he or she has accumulated.

After these comments on the five categories of elements of gamification in education identified by Toda et al. (2019) and with the aim of concluding this subheading regarding the elements of gamification, we present some reflections in this regard. First, we should bear in mind the fact that some elements can be sorted into more than one category. For example, leaderboards, which fall into the category of social elements because they allow comparisons between users, also provide feedback to students regarding their performance (Cao et al., 2022). Therefore, they could also be included in the performance/measurement category. A similar situation is relevant to sensations. Although Toda et al. (2019) categorize sensations as personal elements, they are related to the narrative of the experience and are aimed at promoting the immersion of the participants. Therefore, they fall between this category and the fictional category.

Second, it should be noted that some elements that are intended to create a certain type of environment—competitive or collaborative—may not have the desired effect. For example, leaderboards facilitate comparison and encourage competition among participants (Toda et al., 2019). However, the study conducted by Zahedi et al. (2021) reports the testimony of one student who claims that leaderboards do not influence her since she does not know her classmates. In the university environment, classes are usually composed of a large number of students. Moreover, unlike the situation in lower levels of education, all students do not share the same subjects as they may be enrolled in different courses and in different years of their education. In this context, some students may not have any links with their classmates.

In such a scenario, as discussed in the work of Zahedi et al. (2021), gamification elements aimed at creating a competitive environment may not have any effect on participants who have no relationship with their peers. Therefore, these authors suggest that the use of leaderboards may be more effective in small classes featuring a sense of community, as this approach can facilitate competition since students who occupy higher positions on the leaderboard feel rewarded.

These results encourage us to reflect on the elements that are more favorable in the particular conditions in which we intend to develop our gamified activity. As previously mentioned, the available elements do not represent a final list. Likewise, their effects depend on the circumstances in which the activity is implemented. For this reason, the position of the analysis phase prior to the conception of the gamified experience is of great importance.

2.3.2.2 Duration

Studies show that the effects of gamification on users differ over time, with the impact varying in accordance with the duration of the gamified experience. The presentation of and participation in the gamified activity in its initial moments are attractive due to its novelty, a phenomenon which is known as the novelty effect (Hamari et al., 2014; Miguel-Alonso et al., 2023). Individuals seem to prefer intense activities that offer rewards in the short term (Kim & Castelli, 2021). This preference is closely linked to extrinsic motivation: users participate with the aim of receiving something in return, in this case, the rewards offered by the gamified activity, such as points or badges.

The main challenge faced by the designers of gamified systems is the need to maintain the interest of participants over time. To overcome this challenge, they must create meaningful experiences that learners perceive as useful (Tsay et al., 2020). The lack of student engagement may be due to several reasons, primarily including engagement with other subjects taken by the students and forgetfulness (Tsay et al., 2020). If we want to create an activity that is interesting in the long term, we must introduce elements that generate intrinsic motivation (Koivisto & Hamari, 2019; Srivastava et al., 2023). In this way, we can encourage learners to participate and engage due to the way in which the activity itself provides entertainment and generates interest.

Rodrigues et al. (2022) investigate the variation in the effects of gamification on university students over time and analyze its form. These authors find that the initial effects of gamification decrease over time (i.e., the novelty effect) and subsequently increase until they reach their initial levels. In other words, the impact of gamification seems to follow a U-shaped curve. Specifically, Rodrigues et al. (2022) note that this decrease begins after four weeks and that the subsequent increase takes place between the sixth and tenth week after the start of the activity. The latter phenomenon is referred to as the familiarization effect. This effect refers to the re-emergence of the impact of gamification without any modification in the design of the experience, and it occurs due to the familiarization of the students with the activity.

When devising the design, we can decide whether to gamify the whole of a subject or to include one or more gamified activities in the course. Another option is to use levels or a combination of activities with different lengths. As mentioned, levels divide a gamified activity into several phases and are indicative of the learner's progress (van der Lubbe et al., 2021). We can introduce different levels to our activity to differentiate different stages within the activity in an attempt to maintain the learners' interest throughout the activity's duration by preventing it from becoming monotonous.

Likewise, the other alternative we mentioned is the combination of activities with different durations throughout the course. Chans and Portuguez Castro (2021) develop a gamified design featuring activities of long, medium, and short duration and apply it to two subjects related to chemistry. These activities are based on the use of points and badges to motivate students. Specifically, in the context of these long-duration activities, points are awarded to students based on their attendance and participation in class throughout the course. With respect to the medium-length activities, the points that students are able to receive depend on the completion of homework assignments and the grades they obtain. Unlike long-term activities, these medium-term activities are one-time activities. Finally, short-duration activities offer badges to students. At the end of each class, the teacher determines the distribution of badges. Due to this design, students are motivated, and they are familiar with the objectives that they must achieve in the short, medium, and long term to obtain rewards (Chans & Portuguez Castro, 2021).

2.3.2.3 Platforms

The introduction of gamification to a course can be accomplished in different ways. In general, we differentiate between applications that make use of technology and those that do not. Using technology can facilitate this task and create experiences with which learners can connect more easily. As mentioned, the current generation of students is more likely to adopt new educational technologies than the previous generation (Kuleto et al., 2021), and the current generation also exhibits a preference for virtual learning environments (Vizcaya-Moreno & Pérez-Cañaveras, 2020; Hwang et al., 2023).

In the case of the introduction of gamification via technological means, teachers can either rely on preexisting platforms or develop their own platforms. Preexisting platforms represent a simple resource that can be used by the teacher without requiring too much computer knowledge since such platforms have already been created. Developing one's own platform, on the other hand, requires more effort. Nadi-Ravandi and Batooli's (2022) study of gamification in education identifies the following platforms as the most frequently used: Kahoot, ClassDojo, Duolingo, Moodle, Quizziz, and Khan. However, at present, many more platforms allow us to introduce gamification to a course, such as Socrative, Zondle, and Quizbot. Gamification can also be employed via the learning management systems used in educational institutions, such as Moodle and Blackboard (Nadi-Ravandi & Batooli, 2022; Alzahrani & Alhalafawy, 2023).

Rivera (2019) identifies three uses of the ClassDojo platform: it allows students to track their academic behavior, facilitates collaborative work, and promotes their engagement. Socrative, Kahoot, and Quizizz are examples of gamified educational platforms whose purpose is to administer quizzes. These applications are similar to one another. Therefore, it is unsurprising that these platforms are sometimes used interchangeably to accomplish the same purpose (e.g., Durrani et al., 2022; Janković et al., 2023).

All of these platforms allow quizzes to be created easily and encourage competition among students by including elements such as points and leaderboards. They represent a resource that facilitates the introduction of gamification to the classroom since teachers are only required to enter the questions and answers on the platform, which is perhaps the reason why quizzes are the most frequent element of gamified activities in higher education (Saxena & Mishra, 2021).

These platforms can be used, for example, to carry out evaluations prior to the explanation of the syllabus to assess the students' degree of prior knowledge. If these platforms are used after the question has been seen and explained by the teacher, an evaluation can be executed to establish the degree of knowledge students have acquired (Khairul Anhar Holder et al., 2022; Perera & Hervás-Gómez, 2021).

In the context of distance learning higher education, these quiz-based gamified applications can help ensure student engagement (Rivas-García & Magadán-Díaz, 2022). The COVID-19 pandemic forced the transfer of classes to the virtual environment. During this period, both teachers and students were required to adapt to this new reality and to overcome the challenge of using digital media without possessing the necessary skills (Reyna-Figueroa et al., 2020). Additionally, the combination of this change from face-to-face to distance learning with confinement negatively affected the performance of university students (Kecojevic et al., 2020; Di Pietro, 2023).

In this context, gamified quiz platforms can be very useful, as they can improve student participation and motivation in classes that are taught remotely (Rivas-García and Magadán-Díaz, 2022). It should be noted that the use of these platforms in the particular case of teaching future teachers serves as an example of future practices that these future teachers can use in their roles in the working world (Rivera, 2019; Vankúš, 2023).

After discussing the characteristics of the main preexisting platforms, we will examine proprietary platforms. The development of a proprietary platform offers certain advantages over the use of existing platforms. The most obvious such advantage is that the platform can be adapted to the activity in question due to the ability to add as many elements and functionalities as the designer wishes as well as the ability to make decisions regarding the platform's visual appearance. For example, according to a study conducted by Santos et al. (2023), the color used in the design seems to affect student performance in the case of gamified educational platforms (Santos et al., 2023).

However, the development of a proprietary platform faces several obstacles. The first of these obstacles is the complexity of creating such a platform since it is usually necessary to possess technical knowledge to be able to accomplish this task. However, some resources are available to facilitate this task. For example, the MIT App Inventor is a free resource that allows applications to be created in a few minutes and that facilitates the addition of gamified designs can be added, as shown in the study conducted by Areed et al. (2021). The second obstacle is the time required by this task. For example, Chapman and Rich (2018) design and develop their own platform, which integrates 15 elements of gamification and, according to their results, offers a more motivating educational experience than traditional classes. This duration of this phase prior to its use with students was more than two years.

After examining the way in which a gamified activity is conceived and developed in detail, we discuss in the following subsection the final step in the gamification process: the implementation and evaluation of the activity.

2.3.3 Implementation and Evaluation

After analyzing the context in which the gamified activity is to be implemented and designing the experience, the next step is to implement the activity. First, it is advisable to conduct a pilot study to verify that the gamified activity is implemented properly and that the desired objectives are thus achieved (Krath et al., 2021; Lv, 2023). If this situation is not the case, problems can be recognized, and amendments can be made to improve the experience.

Subsequently, we implement the activity in relation to students. In this final step, we must bear in mind that the gamified design is flexible and that we can modify it. In particular, we must monitor its correct development throughout the course of the activity (Deterding, 2015). In such a case, if we detect any anomaly in the operation or the interim results are not as expected, we can adjust the design to try to improve it. That is, we are not required to wait for the activity to end to evaluate its effects. In contrast, we should perform checks as the activity is ongoing.

It is also recommended to conduct a more exhaustive evaluation of the results once the gamified experience comes to an end. The objective of this evaluation is to analyze possible errors in detail and to consider the improvements that can be made to the design. For example, Bai et al. (2022) report in their study the ways in which they improved their gamified activity after evaluating its results. Specifically, these authors analyzed the effects of gamification on university students in an e-learning course over the course of a semester. They created an experience based on several elements: goals, access, feedback, challenge, and collaboration. After analyzing the results, they concluded that gamification promoted student engagement during the beginning of the activity but that students' interest decreased over the following weeks. To improve the design, these authors decided to introduce a new element: fantasy. This new activity was developed over the course of another semester, in which context it was found that this new version was able to promote interaction among students, their performance, and the quality of the educational experience more effectively than the initial experience.

With this step, we conclude the section concerning the steps involved in the process of gamifying an activity. In the following section, we explore the possibilities of combining gamification with other methodologies in the context of higher education.

2.4 Gamification and Other Methodologies

Gamification can be combined with other educational methodologies and resources to create more enriching experiences. Next, we discuss two of them: flipped classroom and problem-based learning. However, it should be noted that gamification can be combined with many more methodologies and resources, such as augmented reality (Lampropoulos et al., 2022; Petrovych et al., 2023). To this end, designers of gamified experiences must analyze the characteristics of the activity, consider how to introduce gamification, and evaluate the results it provides.

2.4.1 Flipped Classroom

The flipped classroom methodology consists of converting the traditional lectures in which the teacher explains the theoretical contents inside the classroom into work that the student must previously carry out outside the classroom. In this way, students are prepared to carry out the activities proposed in class (Galindo-Dominguez, 2021; Hew et al., 2021; Jia et al., 2023).

Ekici (2021) reviewed the combination of gamification and flipped classrooms. His most relevant findings are the following. First, the most commonly used elements in this context are points, badges, and leaderboards. These items are common in both this and other areas (Oppong-Tawiah et al., 2020). Second, the most commonly used platforms for introducing gamification are learning management systems such as Moodle and Blackboard. Other studies include educational platforms that aim to conduct quizzes, such as Kahoot (Ekici, 2021). Finally, Ekici (2021) concludes that most studies on gamification and flipped classroom combination show that gamification improves students' motivation and academic performance in this specific context.

For example, the study by Murillo-Zamorano et al. (2021) empirically demonstrates that gamification favors the development of university students' skills without harming their satisfaction or their final grades in an active learning environment in which the flipped classroom methodology is included. Sailer and Sailer (2021) introduce gamification in the in-class activities of their experience based on the flipped classroom methodology and obtain that this technique has a positive effect on students' performance and motivation.

2.4.2 Project-Based Learning

Project-based learning is "an instructional approach that allows active engagement in authentic investigation of real-life and open-ended problems, in the form of small groups" (Barak & Yuan, 2021, p. 2). It can be applied in different ways in higher education, and in this field, its use is recommended to promote critical thinking and self-directed learning applied to problem-solving (Li et al., 2022; Loyens et al., 2023).

Abdul Ghani et al. (2022) conducted a systematic review of gamification in activities under the project-based learning methodology and differentiated six main themes: high-fidelity simulation, inquisitive exploration, collaborative learning, interactive instruction, guidance and feedback, and rewards. Concerning high-fidelity simulation, gamification makes it possible to introduce role-play and create realistic scenarios to develop the problem-based learning activity. Inquisitive exploration relates to the ability of gamification to promote student curiosity and create a positive learning environment that encourages students to explore.

In collaborative learning, gamification can be used to establish the dynamics between different groups of learners, as well as cooperation between groups and competition between them. Through various tools, gamification can make instruction more interactive, creating challenges and using narrative to give meaning to the experience (Abdul Ghani et al., 2022).

As earlier stated, gamification can be used to provide feedback to learners. This can also be applied when developing a gamified activity in a problem-based learning environment. Likewise, gamification can provide guidance by knowing the objectives and the structure they will follow. Finally, Abdul Ghani et al. (2022) refer to the ability of gamification to provide rewards in this environment. These rewards can be instantaneous and associated with a specific task.

In short, gamification is a technique that can be incorporated into higher education in methodologies and resources such as flipped classroom and project-based learning. However, there are more methodologies and educational resources that can be combined with gamification. This book deals with gamification and design thinking in higher education. Therefore, the next chapter is dedicated to design thinking, including case study examples.

References

Abdul Ghani, A. S., Abdul Rahim, A. F., Yusoff, M. S. B., & Hadie, S. N. H. (2022). Developing an interactive PBL environment via persuasive gamify elements: A scoping review. *Research and Practice in Technology Enhanced Learning, 17*, 21.

Ahmad, A., Zeeshan, F., Marriam, R., Samreen, A., & Ahmed, S. (2021). Does one size fit all? Investigating the effect of group size and gamification on learners' behaviors in higher education. *Journal of Computing in Higher Education, 33*(2), 296–327.

Albertazzi, D., Ferreira, M. G. G., & Forcellini, F. A. (2019). A wide view on gamification. *Technology, Knowledge and Learning, 24*(2), 191–202.

Alvarez, J., & Djaouti, D. (2011). An introduction to serious game definitions and concepts. *Serious Games & Simulation for Risks Management, 11*(1), 11–15.

Alzahrani, F. K., & Alhalafawy, W. S. (2023). Gamification for learning sustainability in the blackboard system: Motivators and obstacles from faculty members' perspectives. *Sustainability, 15*(5), 4613.

Anunpattana, P., Khalid, M. N. A., Iida, H., & Inchamnan, W. (2021). Capturing potential impact of challenge-based gamification on gamified quizzing in the classroom. *Heliyon, 7*(12).

Areed, M. F., Amasha, M. A., Abougalala, R. A., Alkhalaf, S., & Khairy, D. (2021). Developing gamification e-quizzes based on an android app: The impact of asynchronous form. *Education and Information Technologies, 26*, 4857–4878.

Ayastuy, M. D., Torres, D., & Fernández, A. (2021). Adaptive gamification in collaborative systems, a systematic mapping study. *Computer Science Review, 39*, 100333.

Bagheri, A., Alinezhad, A., & Sajadi, S. M. (2020). Entrepreneurship education and gamification: An analysis of students' learning outcomes. In *The entrepreneurial behaviour: Unveiling the cognitive and emotional aspect of entrepreneurship* (pp. 25–39). Bingley: Emerald Publishing Limited.

Bai, S., Hew, K. F., Gonda, D. E., Huang, B., & Liang, X. (2022). Incorporating fantasy into gamification promotes student learning and quality of online interaction. *International Journal of Educational Technology in Higher Education, 19*, 29.

Baptista, G., & Oliveira, T. (2019). Gamification and serious games: A literature meta-analysis and integrative model. *Computers in Human Behavior, 92*, 306–315.

Barak, M., & Yuan, S. (2021). A cultural perspective to project-based learning and the cultivation of innovative thinking. *Thinking Skills and Creativity, 39*, 100766.

Barata, G., Gama, S., Jorge, J., & Gonçalves, D. (2017). Studying student differentiation in gamified education: A long-term study. *Computers in Human Behavior, 71*, 550–585.

Bartle, R. (1996). *Hearts, clubs, diamonds, spades: Players who suit MUDs.* Recuperado de. http://mud.co.uk/richard/hcds.htm

Bennani, S., Maalel, A., & Ben Ghezala, H. (2022). Adaptive gamification in E-learning: A literature review and future challenges. *Computer Applications in Engineering Education, 30*(2), 628–642.

Bizzi, L. (2023). Why to gamify performance management? Consequences of user engagement in gamification. *Information & Management, 60*(3), 103762.

Bouchrika, I., Harrati, N., Wanick, V., & Wills, G. (2021). Exploring the impact of gamification on student engagement and involvement with e-learning systems. *Interactive Learning Environments, 29*(8), 1244–1257.

Bovermann, K., & Bastiaens, T. J. (2020). Towards a motivational design? Connecting gamification user types and online learning activities. *Research and Practice in Technology Enhanced Learning, 15*, 1.

Cao, Y., Gong, S. Y., Wang, Z., Cheng, Y., & Wang, Y. Q. (2022). More challenging or more achievable? The impacts of difficulty and dominant goal orientation in leaderboards within educational gamification. *Journal of Computer Assisted Learning, 38*(3), 845–860.

Cechella, F., Abbad, G., & Wagner, R. (2021). Leveraging learning with gamification: An experimental case study with bank managers. *Computers in Human Behavior Reports, 3*, 100044.

Cechetti, N. P., Bellei, E. A., Biduski, D., Rodriguez, J. P. M., Roman, M. K., & De Marchi, A. C. B. (2019). Developing and implementing a gamification method to improve user engagement: A case study with an m-Health application for hypertension monitoring. *Telematics and Informatics, 41*, 126–138.

Chan, V., & Baig, S. (2023). Level up: Gamifying medical education for enhanced learning experiences. *The American Journal of the Medical Sciences, 366*(4), 243–244.

Chans, G. M., & Portuguez Castro, M. (2021). Gamification as a strategy to increase motivation and engagement in higher education chemistry students. *Computers, 10*(10), 132.

Chapman, J. R., & Rich, P. J. (2018). Does educational gamification improve students' motivation? If so, which game elements work best? *Journal of Education for Business, 93*(7), 315–322.

Cheng, Z., Wang, H., Zhu, X., West, R. E., Zhang, Z., & Xu, Q. (2023). Open badges support goal setting and self-efficacy but not self-regulation in a hybrid learning environment. *Computers & Education, 197*, 104744.

Cömert, Z., & Samur, Y. (2021). A comprehensive player types model: Player head. *Interactive Learning Environments, 31*(5), 2930–2946.

Csíkszentmihályi, M. (1975). *Beyond boredom and anxiety.* San Francisco, CA: Jossey-Bass.

Csíkszentmihályi, M. (1990). *Flow: The psychology of optimal experience.* New York: Harper & Row.

da Silva Júnior, J. N., Castro, G. D. L., Melo Leite Junior, A. J., Monteiro, A. J., & Alexandre, F. S. O. (2022). Gamification of an entire introductory organic chemistry course: A strategy to enhance the students' engagement. *Journal of Chemical Education, 99*(2), 678–687.

Deci, E., & Ryan, R. M. (1985). *Intrinsic motivation and self-determination in human behavior.* New York: Springer Science & Business Media.

Deci, E. L., & Ryan, R. M. (2000). The" what" and" why" of goal pursuits: Human needs and the self-determination of behavior. *Psychological Inquiry, 11*(4), 227–268.

Dehghanzadeh, H., Farrokhnia, M., Dehghanzadeh, H., Taghipour, K., & Noroozi, O. (2023). Using gamification to support learning in K-12 education: A systematic literature review. *British Journal of Educational Technology, 00*: 1–37.

de la Peña, D., Lizcano, D., & Martínez-Álvarez, I. (2021). Learning through play: Gamification model in university-level distance learning. *Entertainment Computing*, *39*, 100430.

Denden, M., Tlili, A., Chen, N. S., Abed, M., Jemni, M., & Essalmi, F. (2022). The role of learners' characteristics in educational gamification systems: A systematic meta-review of the literature. *Interactive Learning Environments*, 1–23.

Denden, M., Tlili, A., Essalmi, F., Jemni, M., Chang, M., & Huang, R. (2019). Imoodle: An intelligent gamified moodle to predict "at-risk" students using learning analytics approaches. In *Data analytics approaches in educational games and gamification systems* (pp. 113–126). Singapore: Springer.

Denden, M., Tlili, A., Essalmi, F., Jemni, M., Chen, N. S., & Burgos, D. (2021). Effects of gender and personality differences on students' perception of game design elements in educational gamification. *International Journal of Human-Computer Studies*, *154*, 102674.

Deterding, S. (2015). The lens of intrinsic skill atoms: A method for gameful design. *Human–Computer Interaction*, *30*(3–4), 294–335.

Deterding, S., Dixon, D., Khaled, R., & Nacke, L. (2011, September). From game design elements to gamefulness: Defining gamification. In *Proceedings of the 15th international academic MindTrek conference: Envisioning future media environments* (pp. 9–15). Tampere, Finland: ACM.

Díaz-Ramírez, J. (2020). Gamification in engineering education–an empirical assessment on learning and game performance. *Heliyon*, *6*(9), e04972.

Dichev, C., Dicheva, D., & Irwin, K. (2020). Gamifying learning for learners. *International Journal of Educational Technology in Higher Education*, *17*, 54.

Diefenbach, S., & Müssig, A. (2019). Counterproductive effects of gamification: An analysis on the example of the gamified task manager Habitica. *International Journal of Human-Computer Studies*, *127*, 190–210.

Di Pietro, G. (2023). The impact of Covid-19 on student achievement: Evidence from a recent meta-analysis. *Educational Research Review*, *39*, 100530.

Duggal, K., Singh, P., & Gupta, L. R. (2021). Impact of gamification, games, and game elements in education. In *Innovations in information and communication technologies (IICT-2020)* (pp. 201–210). Cham: Springer.

Durrani, U. K., Al Naymat, G., Ayoubi, R. M., Kamal, M. M., & Hussain, H. (2022). Gamified flipped classroom versus traditional classroom learning: Which approach is more efficient in business education? *The International Journal of Management Education*, *20*(1), 100595.

Ekici, M. (2021). A systematic review of the use of gamification in flipped learning. *Education and Information Technologies*, *26*(3), 3327–3346.

Faust, A. (2021). Literature and theoretical background of gamification. In *The effects of gamification on motivation and performance* (pp. 7–44). Wiesbaden: Springer Gabler.

Featherstone, M., & Habgood, J. (2019). UniCraft: Exploring the impact of asynchronous multiplayer game elements in gamification. *International Journal of Human-Computer Studies*, *127*, 150–168.

Ferriz-Valero, A., Østerlie, O., García Martínez, S., & García-Jaén, M. (2020). Gamification in physical education: Evaluation of impact on motivation and academic performance within higher education. *International Journal of Environmental Research and Public Health*, *17*(12), 4465.

Floryan, M., Chow, P. I., Schueller, S. M., & Ritterband, L. M. (2020). The model of gamification principles for digital health interventions: Evaluation of validity and potential utility. *Journal of Medical Internet Research*, *22*(6), e16506.

Floryan, M. R., Ritterband, L. M., & Chow, P. I. (2019). Principles of gamification for Internet interventions. *Translational Behavioral Medicine*, *9*(6), 1131–1138.

Fontana, M. T. (2020). Gamification of ChemDraw during the COVID-19 pandemic: Investigating how a serious, educational-game tournament (molecule madness) impacts student wellness and organic chemistry skills while distance learning. *Journal of Chemical Education*, *97*(9), 3358–3368.

Galindo-Dominguez, H. (2021). Flipped classroom in the educational system. *Educational Technology & Society*, *24*(3), 44–60.

González-González, C. S., Toledo-Delgado, P. A., Muñoz-Cruz, V., & Arnedo-Moreno, J. (2022). Gender and age differences in preferences on game elements and platforms. *Sensors*, *22*(9), 3567.

Hamari, J., Koivisto, J., & Sarsa, H. (2014, January). Does gamification work?–A literature review of empirical studies on gamification. In *Proceedings of the 2014 47th Hawaii international conference on system sciences* (pp. 3025–3034). IEEE Computer Society Conference Publishing Services (CPS). Waikoloa, HI, USA.

Harman, J. L., & Brown, K. D. (2022). Illustrating a narrative: A test of game elements in game-like personality assessment. *International Journal of Selection and Assessment*, *30*(1), 157–166.

Hervás, R., Ruiz-Carrasco, D., Mondéjar, T., & Bravo, J. (2017, May). Gamification mechanics for behavioral change: A systematic review and proposed taxonomy. In *Proceedings of the 11th EAI international conference on pervasive computing technologies for healthcare* (pp. 395–404). Association for Computing Machinery. Barcelona, Spain.

Hew, K. F., Bai, S., Dawson, P., & Lo, C. K. (2021). Meta-analyses of flipped classroom studies: A review of methodology. *Educational Research Review*, *33*, 100393.

Hsu, C. L. (2022). Applying cognitive evaluation theory to analyze the impact of gamification mechanics on user engagement in resource recycling. *Information & Management*, *59*(2), 103602.

Hunicke, R., LeBlanc, M., & Zubek, R. (2004, July). MDA: A formal approach to game design and game research. *Proceedings of the AAAI Workshop on Challenges in Game AI*, *4*(1), 1722.

Huotari, K., & Hamari, J. (2017). A definition for gamification: Anchoring gamification in the service marketing literature. *Electronic Markets*, *27*(1), 21–31.

Hwang, C., Ghalachyan, A., & Song, S. (2023). Exploring student experiences with a virtual learning environment in an apparel and textiles curriculum during the COVID-19 pandemic. *International Journal of Fashion Design, Technology and Education*, 1–10.

Janković, A., Maričić, M., & Cvjetićanin, S. (2023). Comparing science success of primary school students in the gamified learning environment via Kahoot and Quizizz. *Journal of Computers in Education*, 1–24.

Jia, C., Hew, K. F., Jiahui, D., & Liuyufeng, L. (2023). Towards a fully online flipped classroom model to support student learning outcomes and engagement: A 2-year design-based study. *The Internet and Higher Education*, *56*, 100878.

Jodoi, K., Takenaka, N., Uchida, S., Nakagawa, S., & Inoue, N. (2021). Developing an active-learning app to improve critical thinking: Item selection and gamification effects. *Heliyon*, *7*(11), e08256.

Jonassen, D. H., & Rohrer-Murphy, L. (1999). Activity theory as a framework for designing constructivist learning environments. *Educational Technology Research and Development*, *47*(1), 61–79.

Kam, A. H., & Umar, I. N. (2023). Fostering autonomous motivation: A deeper evaluation of gamified learning. *Journal of Computing in Higher Education*, 1–21.

Kecojevic, A., Basch, C. H., Sullivan, M., & Davi, N. K. (2020). The impact of the COVID-19 epidemic on mental health of undergraduate students in New Jersey, cross-sectional study. *PLoS ONE*, *15*(9), e0239696.

Keepers, M., Nesbit, I., Romero, D., & Wuest, T. (2022). Current state of research & outlook of gamification for manufacturing. *Journal of Manufacturing Systems*, *64*, 303–315.

Khairul Anhar Holder, N. A., Foong, C. C., & Nik Nazri, N. N. (2022). Gamification of education and peer tutoring: Using Socrative for group-based assessment of knowledge and behaviour. In *Alternative assessments in Malaysian higher education* (pp. 251–257). Singapore: Springer.

Khaldi, A., Bouzidi, R., & Nader, F. (2023). Gamification of e-learning in higher education: A systematic literature review. *Smart Learning Environments*, *10*, 10.

Kim, J., & Castelli, D. M. (2021). Effects of gamification on behavioral change in education: A meta-analysis. *International Journal of Environmental Research and Public Health*, *18*(7), 3550.

Klock, A. C. T., Gasparini, I., Pimenta, M. S., & Hamari, J. (2020). Tailored gamification: A review of literature. *International Journal of Human-Computer Studies*, *144*, 102495.

Koivisto, J., & Hamari, J. (2019). The rise of motivational information systems: A review of gamification research. *International Journal of Information Management*, *45*, 191–210.

Kolb, D. A. (1984). *Experience as the source of learning and development*. Upper Saddle River, NJ: Prentice Hall.

Krath, J., Schürmann, L., & Von Korflesch, H. F. (2021). Revealing the theoretical basis of gamification: A systematic review and analysis of theory in research on gamification, serious games and game-based learning. *Computers in Human Behavior*, *125*, 106963.

Kuleto, V., Stanescu, M., Ranković, M., Šević, N. P., Păun, D., & Teodorescu, S. (2021). Extended reality in higher education, a responsible innovation approach for generation y and generation z. *Sustainability*, *13*(21), 11814.

Lampropoulos, G., Keramopoulos, E., Diamantaras, K., & Evangelidis, G. (2022). Augmented reality and gamification in education: A systematic literature review of research, applications, and empirical studies. *Applied Sciences*, *12*(13), 6809.

Laor, T. (2022). My social network: Group differences in frequency of use, active use, and interactive use on Facebook, Instagram and Twitter. *Technology in Society*, *68*, 101922.

Li, N., Lim, E. G., Leach, M., Zhang, X., & Song, P. (2022). Role of perceived self-efficacy in automated project allocation: Measuring university students' perceptions of justice in interdisciplinary project-based learning. *Computers in Human Behavior*, *136*, 107381.

Liu, D., Santhanam, R., & Webster, J. (2017). Toward meaningful engagement: A framework for design and research of gamified information systems. *MIS Quarterly*, *41*(4), 1011–1034.

Loyens, S. M., Van Meerten, J. E., Schaap, L., & Wijnia, L. (2023). Situating higher-order, critical, and critical-analytic thinking in problem-and project-based learning environments: A systematic review. *Educational Psychology Review*, *35*(2), 39.

Lv, J. (2023). Improving college student engagement and motivation in a gamified learning environment: The pilot study in China. *Current Psychology*, 1–19.

Mavroeidi, A. G., Kitsiou, A., Kalloniatis, C., & Gritzalis, S. (2019). Gamification vs. privacy: Identifying and analysing the major concerns. *Future Internet, 11*(3), 67.

Mazarakis, A., & Bräuer, P. (2023). Gamification is working, but which one exactly? Results from an experiment with four game design elements. *International Journal of Human–Computer Interaction, 39*(3), 612–627.

Miguel-Alonso, I., Rodriguez-Garcia, B., Checa, D., & Bustillo, A. (2023). Countering the novelty effect: A tutorial for immersive virtual reality learning environments. *Applied Sciences, 13*(1), 593.

Milanesi, M., Guercini, S., & Runfola, A. (2022). Let's play! Gamification as a marketing tool to deliver a digital luxury experience. *Electronic Commerce Research.* https://doi.org/10.1007/s10660-021-09529-1

Murillo-Zamorano, L. R., López-Sánchez, J. Á., Godoy-Caballero, A. L., & Bueno-Muñoz, C. (2021). Gamification and active learning in higher education: Is it possible to match digital society, academia and students' interests? *International Journal of Educational Technology in Higher Education, 18*, 15.

Murillo-Zamorano, L. R., López-Sánchez, J. A., López-Rey, M. J., & Bueno-Muñoz, C. (2023). Gamification in higher education: The ECOn+ star battles. *Computers & Education, 194*, 104699.

Na, K., & Han, K. (2023). How leaderboard positions shape our motivation: The impact of competence satisfaction and competence frustration on motivation in a gamified crowdsourcing task. *Internet Research, 33*(7), 1–18.

Nadi-Ravandi, S., & Batooli, Z. (2022). Gamification in education: A scientometric, content and co-occurrence analysis of systematic review and meta-analysis articles. *Education and Information Technologies, 27*, 10207–10238.

Navarro, E. R. L., Giorgetti, D., Mas, C. I., & Barone, P. (2023). Gamification improves extrinsic but not intrinsic motivation to learning in undergraduate students: A counterbalanced study. *European Journal of Education and Psychology, 16*(1), 1–18.

Oliveira, W., Hamari, J., Shi, L., Toda, A. M., Rodrigues, L., Palomino, P. T., & Isotani, S. (2023). Tailored gamification in education: A literature review and future agenda. *Education and Information Technologies, 28*(1), 373–406.

Oppong-Tawiah, D., Webster, J., Staples, S., Cameron, A. F., de Guinea, A. O., & Hung, T. Y. (2020). Developing a gamified mobile application to encourage sustainable energy use in the office. *Journal of Business Research, 106*, 388–405.

Pakinee, A., & Puritat, K. (2021). Designing a gamified e-learning environment for teaching undergraduate ERP course based on big five personality traits. *Education and Information Technologies, 26*, 4049–4067.

Pasca, M. G., Renzi, M. F., Di Pietro, L., & Mugion, R. G. (2021). Gamification in tourism and hospitality research in the era of digital platforms: A systematic literature review. *Journal of Service Theory and Practice, 31*(5), 691–737.

Perera, V. H., & Hervás-Gómez, C. (2021). University students' perceptions toward the use of an online student response system in game-based learning experiences with mobile technology. *European Journal of Educational Research, 10*(2), 1009–1022.

Petrovych, O., Zavalniuk, I., Bohatko, V., Poliarush, N., & Petrovych, S. (2023). Motivational readiness of future teachers-philologists to use the gamification with elements of augmented reality in education. *International Journal of Emerging Technologies in Learning, 18*(3), 4–21.

Piaget, J. (1977). *The development of thought: Equilibration of cognitive structures* (A. Rosin, Trans.). New York: Viking.

Pichler, S., Kohli, C., & Granitz, N. (2021). DITTO for Gen Z: A framework for leveraging the uniqueness of the new generation. *Business Horizons, 64*(5), 599–610.

Putz, L. M., Hofbauer, F., & Treiblmaier, H. (2020). Can gamification help to improve education? Findings from a longitudinal study. *Computers in Human Behavior, 110*, 106392.

Ramos Aguiar, L. R., Álvarez Rodríguez, F. J., Madero Aguilar, J. R., Navarro Plascencia, V., Peña Mendoza, L. M., Quintero Valdez, J. R., . . . Lazcano Ortiz, L. E. (2023). Implementing gamification for blind and autistic people with tangible interfaces, extended reality, and universal design for learning: Two case studies. *Applied Sciences, 13*(5), 3159.

Reyna-Figueroa, J., Arce-Salinas, C. A., Martínez-Arredondo, H., & Lehmann-Mendoza, R. (2020). El papel de los estudiantes de medicina en las pandemias. *Revista chilena de infectología, 37*(4), 456–460.

Rincon-Flores, E. G., Mena, J., & López-Camacho, E. (2022). Gamification as a teaching method to improve performance and motivation in tertiary education during COVID-19: A research study from Mexico. *Education Sciences, 12*(1), 49.

Rivas-García, J. I., & Magadán-Díaz, M. (2022). Gamified learning in online teaching through platforms: The use of quizizz. In *International workshop on learning technology for education challenges* (pp. 3–20). Cham: Springer.

Rivera, C. J. (2019). Using ClassDojo as a mechanism to engage and foster collaboration in university classrooms. *College Teaching, 67*(3), 154–159.

Robson, K., Plangger, K., Kietzmann, J. H., McCarthy, I., & Pitt, L. (2015). Is it all a game? Understanding the principles of gamification. *Business Horizons, 58*(4), 411–420.

Rodrigues, L., Pereira, F. D., Toda, A. M., Palomino, P. T., Pessoa, M., Carvalho, L. S. G., . . . Isotani, S. (2022). Gamification suffers from the novelty effect but benefits from the familiarization effect: Findings from a longitudinal study. *International Journal of Educational Technology in Higher Education, 19*, 13.

Sadovets, O., Martynyuk, O., Orlovska, O., Lysak, H., Korol, S., & Zembytska, M. (2022). Gamification in the informal learning space of higher education (in the context of the digital transformation of education). *Postmodern Openings, 13*(1), 330–350.

Saggah, A., Atkins, A. S., & Campion, R. J. (2020, October). A review of gamification design frameworks in education. In *2020 Fourth international conference on intelligent computing in data sciences (ICDS)* (pp. 1–8). IEEE.

Sailer, M., & Homner, L. (2020). The gamification of learning: A meta-analysis. *Educational Psychology Review, 32*, 77–112.

Sailer, M., & Sailer, M. (2021). Gamification of in-class activities in flipped classroom lectures. *British Journal of Educational Technology, 52*(1), 75–90.

Sakharova, L. V., Tishchenko, E. N., Stryukov, M. B., Bukhov, N. V., & Omarova, G. T. (2023). Fuzzy-multiple model of a gamified mobile application "smart home" based on Bartle's classification of players' psychological types. In *Technological trends in the AI economy: International review and ways of adaptation* (pp. 21–32). Singapore: Springer Nature.

Santos, J., Andrade, E., Benevides, K., Silva, K., Nascimento, J., Bittencourt, I., . . . Isotani, S. (2023). Does gender stereotype threat affects the levels of aggressiveness, learning and flow in gamified learning environments?: An experimental study. *Education and Information Technologies, 28*(2), 1637–1662.

Saxena, M., & Mishra, D. K. (2021). Gamification and Gen Z in higher education: A systematic review of literature. International *Journal of Information and Communication Technology Education (IJICTE)*, *17*(4), 1–22.

Scheibe, K., & Zimmer, F. (2022). Gender differences in perception of gamification elements on social live streaming services. In *Research anthology on feminist studies and gender perceptions* (pp. 405–422). IGI Global, Copenhagen, Denmark.

Schöbel, S. M., Janson, A., & Söllner, M. (2020). Capturing the complexity of gamification elements: A holistic approach for analysing existing and deriving novel gamification designs. *European Journal of Information Systems*, *29*(6), 641–668.

Sezgin, S., & Yüzer, T. V. (2022). Analysing adaptive gamification design principles for online courses. *Behaviour & Information Technology*, *41*(3), 485–501.

Sheffler, Z. J., Liu, D., & Curley, S. P. (2020). Ingredients for successful badges: Evidence from a field experiment in bike commuting. *European Journal of Information Systems*, *29*(6), 688–703.

Shi, S., Leung, W. K., & Munelli, F. (2022). Gamification in OTA platforms: A mixed-methods research involving online shopping carnival. *Tourism Management*, *88*, 104426.

Srivastava, M., Shivani, S., & Dutta, S. (2023). Intrinsic rewards and sustainability-oriented entrepreneurial intentions: Reflections from two case studies in India. In *Handbook of research on promoting an inclusive organizational culture for entrepreneurial sustainability* (pp. 131–147). IGI Global, Bogotá, Colombia.

Staller, M. S., & Koerner, S. (2021). Beyond classical definition: The non-definition of gamification. *SN Computer Science*, *2*, 8.

Sweller, J. (1988). Cognitive load during problem solving: Effects on learning. *Cognitive Science*, *12*(2), 257–285.

Szymkowiak, A., Melović, B., Dabić, M., Jeganathan, K., & Kundi, G. S. (2021). Information technology and Gen Z: The role of teachers, the internet, and technology in the education of young people. *Technology in Society*, *65*, 101565.

Tanouri, A., Kennedy, A. M., & Veer, E. (2022). A conceptual framework for transformative gamification services. *Journal of Services Marketing*, *36*(2), 185–200.

Tenório, K., Dermeval, D., Monteiro, M., Peixoto, A., & Silva, A. P. D. (2022). Exploring design concepts to enable teachers to monitor and adapt gamification in adaptive learning systems: A qualitative research approach. *International Journal of Artificial Intelligence in Education*, *32*(4), 867–891.

Toda, A. M., Klock, A. C., Oliveira, W., Palomino, P. T., Rodrigues, L., Shi, L., . . . Cristea, A. I. (2019). Analysing gamification elements in educational environments using an existing Gamification taxonomy. *Smart Learning Environments*, *6*, 16.

Tsay, C. H. H., Kofinas, A. K., Trivedi, S. K., & Yang, Y. (2020). Overcoming the novelty effect in online gamified learning systems: An empirical evaluation of student engagement and performance. *Journal of Computer Assisted Learning*, *36*(2), 128–146.

van der Lubbe, L. M., Gerritsen, C., Klein, M. C. A., & Hindriks, K. V. (2021). Empowering vulnerable target groups with serious games and gamification. *Entertainment Computing*, *38*, 100402.

van Gaalen, A. E., Brouwer, J., Schönrock-Adema, J., Bouwkamp-Timmer, T., Jaarsma, A. D. C., & Georgiadis, J. R. (2021). Gamification of health professions education: A systematic review. *Advances in Health Sciences Education*, *26*(2), 683–711.

Vankúš, P. (2023). Game-based learning and gamification technologies in the preparation of future mathematics teachers. *International Journal of Interactive Mobile Technologies, 17*(11), 53–67.

Vanolo, A. (2018). Cities and the politics of gamification. *Cities, 74,* 320–326.

Vizcaya-Moreno, M. F., & Pérez-Cañaveras, R. M. (2020). Social media used and teaching methods preferred by generation z students in the nursing clinical learning environment: A cross-sectional research study. *International Journal of Environmental Research and Public Health, 17*(21), 8267.

Wang, Y. F., Hsu, Y. F., & Fang, K. (2022). The key elements of gamification in corporate training–The Delphi method. *Entertainment Computing, 40,* 100463.

Wei, Z., Zhang, J., Huang, X., & Qiu, H. (2023). Can gamification improve the virtual reality tourism experience? Analyzing the mediating role of tourism fatigue. *Tourism Management, 96,* 104715.

Werbach, K., & Hunter, D. (2012). *For the win: How game thinking can revolutionize your business.* Philadelphia, PA: Wharton Digital Press.

Wijayaratna, K. P., Hossein Rashidi, T., & Gardner, L. (2023). Adapting to the emergence of generation Z in tertiary education: Application of blended learning initiatives in transport engineering. *Journal of Civil Engineering Education, 149*(3), 05023001.

Wolf, T., Weiger, W. H., & Hammerschmidt, M. (2020). Experiences that matter? The motivational experiences and business outcomes of gamified services. *Journal of Business Research, 106,* 353–364.

Xu, J., Lio, A., Dhaliwal, H., Andrei, S., Balakrishnan, S., Nagani, U., & Samadder, S. (2021). Psychological interventions of virtual gamification within academic intrinsic motivation: A systematic review. *Journal of Affective Disorders, 293,* 444–465.

Yang, H., & Li, D. (2021). Health management gamification: Understanding the effects of goal difficulty, achievement incentives, and social networks on performance. *Technological Forecasting and Social Change, 169,* 120839.

Yastibas, A. E., Baturay, M. H., & Ertas, A. (2021). Gen Zers in higher education: A generational study on generation Z English language learners. *i-Manager's Journal on School Educational Technology, 17*(2), 7–15.

Yen, B. T., Mulley, C., & Burke, M. (2019). Gamification in transport interventions: Another way to improve travel behavioural change. *Cities, 85,* 140–149.

Zahedi, L., Batten, J., Ross, M., Potvin, G., Damas, S., Clarke, P., & Davis, D. (2021). Gamification in education: A mixed-methods study of gender on computer science students' academic performance and identity development. *Journal of Computing in Higher Education, 33*(?), 441–474.

Zainuddin, Z., Chu, S. K. W., Shujahat, M., & Perera, C. J. (2020). The impact of gamification on learning and instruction: A systematic review of empirical evidence. *Educational Research Review, 30,* 100326.

Zecri, E., Ouzzif, M., & El Haddioui, I. (2021, April). Study of the use of gamification elements in e-learning applications. In *Proceedings of the 4th international conference on networking, information systems & security* (pp. 1–5). Association for Computing Machinery. KENITRA AA Morocco.

Zhu, X., Gong, Q., Wang, Q., He, Y., Sun, Z., & Liu, F. (2023). Analysis of students' online learning engagement during the COVID-19 pandemic: A case study of a SPOC-based geography education undergraduate course. *Sustainability, 15*(5), 4544.

3 Design Thinking in Higher Education

3.1 Introduction

Design thinking is a way of solving problems through innovation. The focus of such thinking is on users and solutions rather than on the problem itself. The commitment of design thinking to become involved with the people behind the problem is one characteristic that distinguishes design thinking from other processes of innovation and ideation. In searching for a solution, design thinking asks "Who will be the user?" and "How will this solution impact the user?" In this sense, the most crucial element of design thinking is the development of empathy with stakeholders. If designers understand the people who are affected by a problem, it is possible to find a more impactful solution (Han, 2022).

In the first "World Design Summit," which was held in Montreal in 2017, 14 organizations asked governments, education institutions, civil society, and design professionals to adopt design thinking as an engine for innovation. Ultimately, with the "Montreal Declaration," these organizations sought to follow a design-driven approach to change and improvement that connects technology with human needs in all spheres of life (World Design Summit, 2017).

Design-driven innovation is a concept that was introduced in 2009 by Roberto Verganti, professor at Politecnico di Milano. This concept highlights the way in which design capacity is related to value creation via reshaping processes that offer unexpected solutions. In this conceptualization, designers facilitate the integration of multidisciplinary teams that experiment with ideas, transcend disciplinary boundaries, and combine different technical, organizational, cultural, and communicative abilities (Verganti, 2009; Bakırlıoğlu, 2023).

In this sense, the main value of design thinking is to offer a defined process for innovation: a step-by-step procedure that helps generate a new and useful product, process, service, policy, management model, or business model. However, of course, novelty is already implied by the concept of innovation. What design thinking contributes is a process for ensuring that the solution is

DOI: 10.4324/9781032675558-3

useful to stakeholders (Felder et al., 2023). In this way, design thinking promotes innovation due to the fact that following the concrete steps of design thinking leads to the rise of innovative solutions that are also more meaningful and impactful (Han, 2022; Lemström, 2023). In the remainder of this section, the chapter explores the nature of design thinking in further depth as well as its history and the more relevant models that articulate its process and development.

3.1.1 What Is Design Thinking?

There is no unique definition of design thinking. We believe that it is useful to approach its definition from three different angles: design thinking as a concept, design thinking as a process, and design thinking as a mindset for understanding the world.

Understood as a concept, design thinking can be described as a practical framework for addressing real-world uncertainty. Design thinking uses the designer's sensibility and methods to develop a systematic way of removing bias from the strategic debate regarding what should be done next (Datar, 2022; School). As a concept, it aims to fulfill people's needs by combining the available technology with viable business strategies to generate value for customers and market opportunities (Matthews & Wrigley, 2017; Kurek et al., 2023).

The second approach focuses on design thinking as a process. In this regard, there are many ways to approach problem-solving, of which design thinking is merely one (Han, 2022). From this point of view, design thinking allows the user to develop creative strategies to archetype models, collect reactions, and reformulate initial approaches to the problem (Razzouk & Shute, 2012). Design thinking is a step-by-step recursive process and a method for addressing complex problems (Matthews & Wrigley, 2017; Pope-Ruark et al., 2019).

Third, it is useful to view design thinking as a mindset based on designers' workflows. From this perspective, the purpose of design thinking is to provide professionals with standardized practices that allow them to implement innovation processes. Hence, professionals can develop creative solutions to difficult, complex, or entrenched problems, whether or not they are related to design (Han, 2022; Vendraminelli et al., 2023). As a mindset, design thinking approaches problem-solving and innovation from a humanistic perspective on design. This approach puts people at the center of the design process, and in so doing, it allows the conception of products and services that are adjusted to the needs of end users (Laundry, 2020; Bertão et al., 2023). Using Carol Dweck's terminology (Dweck, 2006), we can say that design thinking implies a growth mindset, which rests on the belief that people can develop their creativity and intelligence by exhibiting persistence in the face of setbacks.

To summarize, Guaman-Quintanilla et al. (2022), based on their review of the literature, propose the following definition of design thinking:

> Design thinking is a way of working and thinking that goes beyond the pure design context, as it is a way of solving ill-defined problems using methods and mindsets typically associated with designers, but adapting them to different real contexts and applying a human-centered and prototype-driven approach, which fosters creativity and promotes the value of teamwork.
>
> (p. 3)

3.1.2 History of Design Thinking

Design thinking is a relatively new method in comparison with other methods for exploring, researching, or inventing. Before becoming mainstream, design thinking was explored by numerous writers. Although some publications on this subject emerged as early as the 1930s, it was only during the 1960s and 1970s when creativity and design researchers from several European and American universities fully developed the notion of design thinking by drawing on industrial processes (Rösch et al., 2023).

Two institutions are key to the origins of design thinking. One of these institutions is IDEO (www.ideo.com/), an international design company whose aim is to have a positive impact on organizations through design (IDEO, 2022a); the other institution is Stanford University (Plattner et al., 2012). These institutions initiated the study and application of this approach in the fields of design innovation, business, and education (Latorre-Cosculluela et al., 2020; Kim et al., 2023).

The origins of IDEO can be traced back to 1978 when David Kelley founded his design firm, David Kelley Design (Kelley & Kelley, 2013). In 1980, Steve Jobs asked Kelley to design a mouse for a new computer. As the previous design was too expensive, the firm updated it by including an easier-to-produce component that is still used in most mechanical mouses.

In 1991, David Kelley merged his company with two other companies to create IDEO Consulting, a firm that is still at the forefront of design thinking today (IDEO, 2022a). Beginning in 2005, with the foundation of Hasso Plattner Institute of Design at Stanford (The "d.school"), design thinking became popularized as a creation tool for collaborative projects.

3.1.3 Models of Design Thinking

What does a design thinking process entail? Throughout the design thinking process, designers engage in several different cognitive processes. Many different models of the steps that users should follow have followed, numbering from three to "n." Despite the differences across models, all of them share some important moments in the process (Latorre-Cosculluela et al., 2020). First, it is necessary to identify the problem that must be solved (Razzouk & Shute, 2012). Second, designers should develop empathy with stakeholders via a deep understanding of their context and reality (Gasca, 2015; Boonkhum, 2023). Finally, designers ideate and develop a potential solution to the proposed challenge that should include an innovative approach to the situation (Kolodner & Wills, 1996).

According to Micheli et al. (2019, p. 131) systematic literature review, there are three "most influential applied models design thinking" developed by the following proponents: IDEO (www.ideo.com/), Stanford Design School (https://dschool.stanford.edu/), and IBM (www.ibm.com/). These organizations develop alternative applied design thinking models structured in different phases of execution. The phases of the IDEO model are the following: Inspiration, Ideation, and Implementation. The Stanford Design School proposes the Stanford d.school model and organized it into five phases: Emphatize, Define, Ideate, Prototype, and Test. Finally, IBM points to the following four phases: Understand, Explore, Prototype, and Evaluate.

Additionally, the literature (Guaman-Quintanilla et al., 2022; Luka, 2019; Ellem, 2018) also points out the fact that design thinking models recently developed share certain elements that are essential to implement a design thinking process: Iteration, convergent-divergent thinking, and flexibility.

Iteration allows designers to conduct additional exploratory research at any stage or to redefine the problem after discovering a new insight while testing an early prototype (Guaman-Quintanilla et al., 2022). Divergent and convergent thinking are both necessary in the design thinking model (Luka, 2019; Efeoğlu & Møller, 2023). Divergent thinking ensures the exploration of various solutions to a problem, while convergent thinking narrows these options to arrive at a final decision. By alternating convergent and divergent thinking, designers can engage in emergent thinking that leads to a new solution.

Finally, flexibility ensures that the process is adapted to the problem and to the specific characteristics of the designers. Any model can be merged with any other model to generate a process that is better suited to the concrete situation at hand. For example, Ellem (2018) elaborates on the model developed by Scheer et al. (2012) by including the same design phases but "connecting them with divergent, convergent and emergent thinking" (Luka, 2019, p. 4). Alternatively, Guaman-Quintanilla et al. (2022) combine the model developed by the Hasso Plattner Institute of Design at Stanford University (the d.school) (2023) with the "double diamond" model (Design Council, 2007), as reported by Santos et al. (2017), thus resulting in six stages instead of the four or five original stages.

The following section focuses on the utility of design thinking in contemporary higher education. Which problems in higher education could be addressed using a design approach? How can this way of thinking help prepare students for the future? Therefore, we examine the skills that students need to succeed in a demanding economic environment. Additionally, we try to convince the reader that design thinking could be a useful tool in higher education.

3.2 Design Thinking in Higher Education

What problems in higher education can be addressed using design thinking? How can this approach help prepare students for the future? In this section, we examine the skills that students need to succeed in a demanding economic environment with the aim of arguing for the use of design thinking in higher education. In higher education, the most traditional teacher-centered approach focuses on the transmission of knowledge (Zhang et al., 2023). In the context of this approach, the curriculum is structured around certain content areas. For each content area, experts organize the topics into modules and divide the knowledge into small chunks that can be taught according to sequential lesson plans for specific academic years (Norman & Spohrer, 1996). In this context, Ken Robinson asks his famous question: "Do schools kill creativity?" (Robinson, 2016). It seems that universities are failing to prepare their students by providing them with the competencies that are often referred to as 21st-century skills. These skills are new abilities that students must possess to integrate their basic skills and knowledge with the implementation of new technologies (Binkley et al., 2012; Lemke, 2002; Southworth et al., 2023).

3.2.1 What Students Should Learn for the 21st Century

In the age of artificial intelligence, big data, and biotechnology, one of the most crucial questions is as follows: What should students learn for the 21st century? (Center for Curriculum Redesign, 2022). This question has several answers, but it seems clear that higher education should focus more on learners and their skills and that teaching should be focused on authentic problems with the aim of promoting creativity and innovative solutions (Dilekçi & Karatay, 2023).

Several institutions coincide in terms of their assessment of the skills needed by students and workers.

The European Centre for the Development of Vocational Training (www.cedefop.europa.eu/en), the European Union (EU) organization that unites everyone with a stake in vocational education and training, analyzed the most frequently requested skills in online job advertisements in the EU27 in 2021. Competencies at the top of the list included working with others (31.0%); accessing and analyzing digital data (23%); using digital tools for collaboration, content creation, and problem-solving (16.4%); solving problems (14.1%); and providing information and support to people (14.0%).

Generally, according to the study results, online job advertisements demand skills (57.4%), knowledge (49.3%), and attitudes and values (48.7%) (Cedefop, 2022).

Likewise, the World Economic Forum (2020) includes problem-solving and creativity among the top five skills in demand in 2025. This orientation is also expressed in a series of EU documents and resolutions, such as "A New Skills Agenda for Europe," "Education and Training 2020" (Council of the European Union, 2009), and "Key Competences for Lifelong Learning" (European Commission, 2018, 2022), in which teamwork, creative and critical thinking, problem-solving, entrepreneurship, innovation, initiative, cultural awareness, and communication are emphasized.

One perspective on competencies for the 21st century is the four-dimensional education model proposed by the Center for Curriculum Redesign (CCR) (Fadel et al., 2015). The four dimensions included in this model are knowledge (what is necessary to know and understand), skills (ways of using that knowledge), character (how to behave and engage in the world), and meta-learning (ways of learning and reflecting on and adapting to change). As Tschepe notes (Tschepe, 2018), design thinking is a powerful tool that supports the final three dimensions: skills, character, and meta-learning.

3.2.2 Why Design Thinking in Higher Education

Design thinking, as a human-centered approach, can help address some of these challenges to higher education in innovative ways. First, design thinking facilitates the development of more up-to-date educational "products," such as new programs, degrees, and modules (Katsumata Shah et al., 2023). For example, Leonard et al. (2016) describe the way in which a working group used a design thinking tool to design a new teacher training professional education program at the University of Canberra (Australia). These authors argue that this approach allows designers to develop the curriculum by reference to much more relevant questions than other strategies (Leonard et al., 2016, p. 3).

Second, this approach supports stakeholders in the creation or redesign of crucial university "services." For example, Mann (2020) describes a process of cocreation using design thinking intended to develop more student-adapted tutoring and support services at the University of Melbourne (Australia). She describes design thinking as an effective method for incorporating student and staff voices into institutional conversations (Mann, 2020, p. 3). The core of this project is the idea that the best way to know how to help or engage students is to ask them about their learning experiences and needs. Therefore, engaging them in a design thinking process allows institutions of higher education to improve support and tutoring services.

Third, design thinking helps foster the 21st-century skills that are in most demand in contemporary labor markets. The integration of design thinking

Design Thinking in Higher Education   43

strategies into universities' curricula can help them develop collaboration and teamwork, creativity, problem-solving, and empathy (Guaman-Quintanilla et al., 2018; Luka, 2019; Scheer et al., 2012).

Razzouk and Shute (2012) and Matthews and Wrigley (2017) review the use of design thinking in higher education programs, finding that many universities expose their students to design thinking in classroom situations and workshops. Beyond Stanford University, other institutions of higher education, such as the University of St. Gallen, the Rotman School of Management at University of Toronto, Politechnico Di Milano, the Lancaster Institute for the Contemporary Arts, the California College of the Arts, the University of Gothenburg, and the University of Technology Sydney, allow students to participate in design thinking in the context of business and management programs. An important question to ask when applying design thinking in education (or in any other field) pertains to whether this approach leads to the development of better, more innovative solutions, that is, whether the products and services that emerge from a process of design thinking are superior to those developed using other approaches. Leonard et al. (2016) highlight this dilemma when they analyze the use of developmental evaluation as a design thinking tool for the development of a new teacher training program. According to these authors, the question of whether the design approach leads to a "better" result will remain open for many years. Only when the graduates of the course establish themselves in professional practice will it be possible to develop a strong sense of the way in which the course has prepared them for practice (Leonard et al., 2016, p. 310).

Hopefully, we have persuaded readers that it would be a good idea to use design thinking; nonetheless, many readers are questioning how they can begin to do so. Therefore, the following section addresses the question of how to plan for such a process beginning with some recommendations that can surely make the beginning of this process easier.

3.3 How to Plan a Design Thinking Process in Higher Education

This section begins with six recommendations for designers initiating a design thinking process in higher education. Subsequently, we consider some necessary elements in the planning of a design thinking process and propose a road map to facilitate teaching with design thinking. Finally, two examples illustrate the way in which this approach works.

3.3.1 Before Beginning

First, it is essential to take diversity into account. Lin and Eichelberger (2020) find that no single design thinking tool is suitable for everyone. Therefore, it is necessary to include a variety of activities, groups, and modes of communication. Interestingly, the question of diversity reinforces the complexity that teachers and instructional designers must face when planning for a teaching-and-learning process. The crucial questions of what works for whom and in what circumstances are key to modern education; we know that teaching and learning designs do not work universally for all learners in all circumstances (Leonard et al., 2016). An instructional design tool that is increasingly used to address this challenge is universal design for learning (UDL), developed by CAST. This educational framework proposes an inclusive and transformative learning process. Its aim is to develop learning settings that address the diverse needs of learners (CAST, 2022).

Second, in a design thinking process, trust among team members is crucial; accordingly, team-building techniques must be part of the process (Kaygan, 2023). Lin and Eichelberger (2020) report that relationship-building activities were the most inspiring or the most fun for a group of faculty members participating in a retreat aimed at redesigning department meetings. Relationship-building techniques may help develop cohesion among group members, and more cohesive groups tend to be more productive (Kerr & Tindale, 2004).

Third, the design thinking experience should support professional or learning development. Participants must understand how activities are organized during the design thinking process and how activities contribute to solving the problem under study. Providing initial information and training regarding the techniques and design thinking itself reduces participants' anxiety, promotes engagement, and leads to more innovative results (Lin & Eichelberger, 2020). Beginning with low-risk tasks helps promote collaboration and consequently improves participants' acceptance of and adjustment to the new way of working (McLaughlan & Lodge, 2019).

Fourth, if university faculty want students to engage in innovative learning activities, they should provide sufficient information regarding the advantages of these activities and their connection to the 21st-century skills that students need to develop. Explaining to students the ways in which design thinking contributes to developing their design and nondesign skills can help convince them to play an active role in this process and increase their willingness to learn design thinking (Han, 2022).

Fifth, some readers may question whether certain design skills can be learned in the classroom. Razzouk and Shute (2012) argue that with sufficient scaffolded practice focusing on meaningful problems and formative feedback, it is possible for students to learn design thinking skills. Pedagogical approaches and instructional designs that involve problem-, project-, and inquiry-based learning can be used to enhance students' design thinking skills (Dym et al., 2005).

Finally, when proposing a design thinking process in the field of higher education (or in any field), it is important to ensure that the proposal is sustainable (Calavia et al., 2023). Participants are normally satisfied with the experience and outcomes of design thinking in higher education. Nevertheless, the time and effort required by these processes is a drawback reported by participants, who ask for meaningful incentives to ensure that team members remain engaged in the process over time (Lin & Eichelberger, 2020). Work overload is a problem not only with respect to engaging faculty in change or redesign processes but also with regard to engaging students in the design thinking experiences included in their courses. Therefore, it is essential to clearly define and communicate to students the weightage of design thinking activities in their overall grade and the manner in which their work is to be assessed.

3.3.2 Planning to Teach Using Design Thinking

Once the design team has considered all these issues and begins to plan for the design thinking activity, it is important to include certain elements in this process. First, the work should be based on a real-world project. The learning challenge should be a problem that is currently relevant, not a textbook exercise. Students benefit from engaging with real challenges and problems that provide them with the opportunity to apply their skills and capacities to real-life scenarios (Ghannam & Chan, 2023).

Second, it is important to address the open-ended nature of these problems. Real-life problems have no single correct solution because they are complex and ambiguous. Engaging with complex problems that have no right answer is a good opportunity for students to practice the 21st-century skills that they need for the workplace. Nevertheless, this situation poses a problem for assessment. It is important to explain clearly the manner in which the process and final product are to be assessed and the weighting of this assessment in the students' final grades.

Finally, as explained, collaborative work is a learning structure that is suitable for a design thinking process (Jiang & Pang, 2023). This principle leads to the use of active learning as the main learning strategy. Hamlin and Janssen (1987) describe active learning as a situation in which the students explore issues under the guidance of the instructor rather than simply listening as the instructor presents facts. Students often view education as a passive process in which instructors are the source of knowledge and students are the receivers of knowledge. Lecture-based courses seem to reinforce this notion. In contrast, the literature suggests that participatory learning is more productive than passive learning. In this type of learning, "the student learns a way of thinking, asking questions, searching for answers, and interpreting observations" (Hamlin & Janssen, 1987, p. 45). This observation brings to mind the key elements of design thinking.

The active learning approach encompasses a broad variety of instructional techniques whose main characteristic is that they are student-centered.

Therefore, active learning designs position students at the center of the learning process in an attempt to engage them in activities, such as reading, writing, discussion, or problem-solving, that promote the analysis, synthesis, and evaluation of class content. Cooperative learning, project- and problem-based learning, and the use of case methods and simulations are approaches that promote active learning (Bonwell & Eison, 1991; Lee et al., 2014).

3.3.3 A Road Map of the Design Thinking Process

Once an educator has chosen a real-world problem to address and selected an instructional structure to frame the design thinking process (as explained, one good option is an active learning approach), he or she must plan activities aimed at accomplishing each step of the design thinking process. In so doing, he or she may find it useful to clarify the "what," "why," and "how" associated with each phase of the design thinking model he or she is using to implement the design thinking process.

For example, the "what" of the empathize phase in the Stanford d.school model consists of learning about the audience for whom the problem is to be solved. The "why" refers to the notion that good solutions are based on people's needs, while the "how" involves watching and listening through observation and engagement. In the same manner, the "what" for the define phase is to research, redefine, and focus on your question or problem. The "why" refers to the belief that the only way to arrive at the right solution is by addressing the right problem. Finally, the "how" associated with framing the right problem expresses this problem as a specific challenge using the question "How might we . . . ?" As for the third phase (the ideate phase), the "what" helps to develop solutions as you combine your understanding of the challenge with your imagination; the "why" takes into account the widest possible range of solutions that maximizes your innovation potential, and the "how" is achieved by brainstorm regarding topics that flow from your challenge statement. The "what" of prototyping phase involves constructing a representation of one or more ideas to show to others. The "why" pertains to the need to facilitate communication with potential users by producing something with which users can interact. The "how" involves generating a prototype that users can experience and subsequently asking them about their experience thereof. Finally, as for the test phase, the "what" implies returning to your original user group and testing your ideas for feedback. The "why" allows us to ask for feedback regarding the prototype as another opportunity to understand the user. As for the "how," it is essential to focus on aspects related to what can be learned from other people while at the same time visualizing potential spaces for generating solutions.

When the educator is clear regarding the "what," "why," and "how" associated with each phase of the design thinking model he or she is using, the next step is to have access to a toolbox that makes it possible to implement the design thinking process and reach its various objectives. The reader interested in going deeper into this area can refer to recent literature (Ungarean et al., 2023; Krolikowski et al., 2022; Selamet, 2023; Lo Presti & Carli, 2023; Nicolai & Thompson, 2023; Fortune et al., 2022; Moretti et al., 2022), and also to several online platforms as, for instance, (a) the collection of resources from the Stanford d.school (https://dschool.stanford.edu/resources), (b) the set of tools from IDEO design kit (www.designkit.org/), (c) the IBM toolkit for enterprise design thinking (www.ibm.com/design/thinking/page/toolkit), (d) the planet resources for design thinking of the Design Council (www.designcouncil.org.uk/our-resources/), (e) the design thinking resources of the Hasso-Plattner-Institute (https://hpi.de/en/school-of-design-thinking/design-thinking/resources.html), (f) the design toolkit of the UOC (http://design-toolkit.uoc.edu/es/), and (g) the tools and toolkit of the Design Thinking Association (www.design-thinking-association.org/explore-design-thinking-topics/design-thinking-toolkits), among others.

3.3.4 Examples of Design Thinking in Higher Education

Most likely, the best way of explaining how to apply design thinking to problems in higher education is the use of examples. In the following section, we provide two hypothetical examples. In the first such example, design thinking is used to explore the ways in which international institutions affect the economy, society, and relations worldwide. Any type of international organization could be the object of this analysis. In the second example, design thinking is used to involve students, teachers, and staff in the process of improving a school, college, or organization. Both examples follow the Stanford d.school model and employ a flipped learning structure.

3.3.4.1 Example 1: "What Can This International Organization Do for You?"

Let us imagine that we are teaching a module for any degree and a certain concrete international organization, institution, or nongovernmental organization (NGO) is relevant to understanding the way in which global relations are organized regarding that concrete topic, for example, World Bank, the International Monetary Fund, the United Nations Organization, the EU, or the World Trade Organization if we think about economic relations, with other possibilities including other environmental, social or developmental organizations such as the World Wildlife Fund, Greenpeace, or the International Labour Organization.

From an instructional design perspective, it is important to choose a teaching strategy that facilitates the design thinking process. One such strategy that is well suited to both design thinking and active learning is the flipped classroom. The Flipped Learning Network defines this instructional style as

> a pedagogical approach in which direct instruction moves from the group learning space to the individual learning space, and the resulting group space is transformed into a dynamic, interactive learning environment where the educator guides students as they apply concepts and engage creatively in the subject matter
>
> (Flipped Learning Network, 2014)

In a flipped classroom, students watch videos outside the classroom to encounter the course material for the first time. In this approach, face-to-face (F2F) time focuses less on content and more on the application of this material to new contexts, higher-level cognitive processing, and collaboration, thereby creating meaningful learning experiences (Bowen, 2012; Fink, 2013).

In our case, the organization in question is the EU, and the context is an "Economics of the European Union" module in a Business and Economics course. The teaching objective is to explore the economic and political logic underlying the European integration process, thus providing the student with a basic understanding of the institutional architecture, current situation, and problems of European economies in the early 21st century. The module focuses its learning outputs on content-specific competencies as well as general skills, such as both individual work and teamwork, to allow students to conduct research, apply their findings to practice, and integrate knowledge; it also emphasizes fluent oral and written communication, critical thinking, and the use of information and communication technologies.

As a final project for the module, we propose an activity entitled "What can the EU do for you?" which features a design thinking process. The main objective of this activity is to make students aware of the impact that EU policies have on the social or economic environment in any context and to help them integrate their technical knowledge of the EU into an understanding of the real-world worries of Europeans. The project uses a flipped learning strategy, thus making it possible to combine in-class with out-of-class work and to alternate individual work with team performance. It may be appropriate to conceptualize this activity as a blended learning experience since there may be insufficient numbers of in-class sessions available to conduct the whole process face to face (Bizami et al., 2023). In this case, it is important to present and explain to students a range of online collaboration tools. This process makes it possible to allow some phases of the activity to take place in a virtual, out-of-class space.

As noted, this design follows the Stanford d.school model and employs a flipped learning structure. The activity begins with a presentation (lasting 1 hour) and an explanation by the educator of the project, its aims, the ways in which it will be carried out, and the manner in which it will be assessed. This approach is important, as it is necessary to clarify to students how the activity will progress, its objectives, and how it is planned. The activity should feature an information sheet containing a basic description of the activity as well as short videos explaining the different steps and what is expected from students. Additionally, it is important to state clearly that individual accountability and group accountability will be combined. Therefore, individual worksheets are compulsory and should be handed in prior to the class sessions. Additionally, the working groups should keep a record of the work they perform (worksheets, post-it notes, minutes, etc.). It would also be useful, considering the high level of difficulty associated with this activity, to ensure that the grade assigned to the activity is weighted sufficiently heavily in students' overall grades to promote student engagement.

During this first F2F session, following the presentation, students define the audience by engaging in a process of brainstorming to identify the group to whom the "you" in the title refers; that is, who are the stakeholders that are impacted by the EU (citizens, customers, firms, families, people of different ages, etc.)? The educator is available to resolve doubts and establish working groups. Each group selects or is assigned a type of stakeholder, that is, a "you." Between sessions, students should conduct individual research regarding the assigned stakeholder, complete a worksheet featuring the stakeholder's main characteristics and relevant data about them, and view a video outlining the next session.

The first session is associated with the empathize phase of the design thinking process (lasting 1–1.5 hours). During this session, the educator monitors the students and resolves doubts. Students complete different group activities. For example, group members pool their knowledge using post-it notes to allow them to download and share their knowledge. The can collaboratively develop an interview guide to obtain more information from objective stakeholders. They can also engage in role play, such that half the team interviews the other half to gain insight into stakeholders' perspectives using the five whys technique.

Between this first session and the subsequent session, if possible, students should interview real-world members of the assigned stakeholder group. Each group member analyzes the interviews individually, identifying two or three problems the stakeholders could face.

The define session (lasting 1 hour) is a crucial moment in the process, so educators should monitor this session, resolve doubts, and help students define the problem properly. Students should begin the work by engaging in a "download your knowledge" activity that asks group members to pool their knowledge using post-it notes and to choose a specific challenge, that is, a concrete aspect of the larger problem to address. The scope of this challenge must be neither too narrow nor too broad. A good way to frame the challenge is to pose it as a "How might we . . . ?" question.

Between sessions, students view a video outlining the following session. Individually, they research the EU's laws, policies, budget, conditions, and so forth that could affect the situation and complete a worksheet summarizing all their individual knowledge.

The third session is devoted to the ideate step in the process (lasting 1 hour). As in the previous sessions, the educator monitors the session, resolves doubts, and proposes a storyboard as the prototype format. Meanwhile, students brainstorm collaboratively and without judgment. Once multiple ideas emerge, students combine them to develop a concrete solution. Group members pool their individual knowledge to allow the group to generate a collective knowledge base. Students conduct more research to specify the EU elements that are relevant to the solution.

As the proposed prototype is a storyboard that the user can use to visualize the whole solution, between the sessions, the students view a video outlining the next session, the main elements of a storyboard, and the resources that are necessary to create a storyboard. During the fourth session (lasting one hour), students create the storyboard and prepare a poster explaining the challenge (the concrete aspect of the problem that they have decided to address) as well as their proposed solution. Meanwhile, the educator monitors the session, resolves doubts, and helps students with the storyboard, especially if they have no previous experience working with this resource.

The period between this session and the following session is important, as students must complete the prototype and the poster. In addition, they must prepare for the final session, in which all of the groups must participate: each group will be assigned a specific stakeholder role to take while participating in a role-playing exercise. To prepare for the role-playing activity, each design group shares with the "stakeholder" their notes regarding that concrete stakeholder type, which they used to develop the solution. At this point, it is very useful for students to view a video outlining the next session so that it is clear what they are expected to do.

This process should feature a final presentation of all the problems explored and the solutions provided. Therefore, the evaluation session, that is, the fifth session (lasting 1–1.5 hours), is based on a role-playing exercise in which each design group presents its prototype of the solution (the storyboard) to the assigned "stakeholder." The stakeholders then use a rubric to assess the solution. Meanwhile, the educator monitors the session, organizes the presentation schedule, provides feedback, and assesses the results. Following the evaluation session, students individually conduct a self-reflection regarding what they have learned throughout the process and jointly analyze their projects using a SWOT (strengths, weaknesses, opportunities, threats) analysis to detect potential areas for improvement. Online collaboration tools can be used to finalize the work.

3.3.4.2 Example 2: "Our School Would Be Much Better If..."

Design thinking can also be used in higher education outside the classroom setting, for example, to improve organization, building use, or other facets of university life that affect diverse stakeholders. Involving students in this process is a logical extension of the theoretical trend toward involving students more thoroughly in the processes of teaching and learning (Matthews & Dollinger, 2023). We are already witnessing an unstoppable trend toward the renewed use of such teaching methods, moving toward more active, student-centered form of learning, in which students are the protagonists in their own learning processes (Gaebel et al., 2018; Weimer, 2002). These students can also contribute to the design of the institutions at which they study (Kennedy & Pek, 2023). Some experts discuss the possibility of increasing the active participation of students in instructional design by transforming their role in decision-making processes (Bahou, 2011; Baroutsis et al., 2016), specifically by increasing their participation in the design of content (Ahmadi & Hasani, 2018) or assessment (Blair & Valdez Noel, 2014).

In our hypothetical example, let us assume that the Dean's Office has called for meetings among administrators, staff, faculty, and students to address the following challenge: "Our School of Business and Economics would be much better if...." Next, we present the design of this activity, including the different phases and the tasks assigned to the participants, in this case, a group of students. Prior to the beginning of the activity, students view two short videos, one of which explains the project, its aims, and the steps involved in completing it, while the other introduces the process of creating a Google Forms survey, a necessary tool to complete the activity. In the first session, that is, the empathize phase, the leader resolves doubts, and establishes working groups. Subsequently, students engage in brainstorming to answer the key question of the project: "What could be improved in the School of Business and Economics?" (study space, collaboration space, timetable, vending machines, water fountains, etc.). Each group selects a topic and constructs a survey to collect students' opinions and feelings regarding that possibility. For example, if the topic in question pertains to a vending machine, students could have different preferences regarding where to install it, what type of food it should contain, and so forth. This activity is based on the authors' teaching experience with respect to the preservice teacher training master's degree at Universidad de Oviedo (Spain). We want to thank the students enrolled during the 2021–22 academic year for their contributions and especially Sofia Buron Santos for generating the initial idea. Between sessions, students use Google Forms to distribute surveys to other students at the school and to collect responses. They must also view a video outlining the following session.

The second session is devoted to the define stage. The leader resolves doubts while students analyze surveys to determine what users would like, organize information, and propose potential solutions. Between sessions, students engage in personal reflection regarding the proposals and view a video explaining how to use a CANVAS model, another tool used to complete the activity. During the third session, that is, the ideate stage, students decide collaboratively which final proposal is to be implemented. With regard to the vending machine, for example, students must select the most desirable characteristics based on users' preferences and recreate the proposal using a CANVAS model.

The subsequent period between sessions is important, as students must obtain some knowledge regarding prototyping. Therefore, they view a video concerning what a prototype is and how one can be created. They should discuss in their working groups the type of prototype that is most suitable for the proposed solution. In the vending machine example, the prototype could be an illustrated blueprint of the machine or a storyboard illustrating how the machine could be integrated into the life of the school. Team members can use online communication tools to complete the work and to organize for the purpose of obtaining the materials necessary to build the prototype. During the prototype session, that is, the fourth session, students create the prototype, and the leader resolves doubts and structures the procedure. In the subsequent between-sessions period, students view an explanatory video regarding the final activity and review information pertaining to the creation of a SWOT analysis, the third tool used during this activity. The final, that is, fifth, session is not an evaluation session, as in the previous example; instead, it is a testing session in which each working group presents its prototype to respond to the question "Our School of Business and Economics would be much better if . . ." in a session that is open to the potential users. The stakeholders vote on the various solutions to generate a ranking and evaluate the projects using a rubric.

After completing the activity, students should individually conduct a self-reflection regarding what they have learned throughout the process and should jointly analyze their projects using a SWOT analysis to detect potential areas for improvement. Online collaboration tools can be used to finalize the work.

Both examples illustrate design thinking in action in the context of higher education. In the first case, the process helps students develop both their design and nondesign skills to propose a creative solution to a real-world problem. In the second case, students construct a community and have the opportunity to express their opinions regarding a shared situation. Giving voice to students using a structured procedure increases their empowerment.

3.4 Higher Education, COVID-19, and Design Thinking

Undoubtedly, any reflection on the future of higher education must take into account the impact of the COVID-19 pandemic. Rob Curtin, in a post published in 2021 on the Educase Review Blog, raised several questions pertaining to the future of higher education after the COVID-19 pandemic: "How has this experience changed expectations? What will emerge as the new normal across campus and in the classroom?" (Curtin, 2021). This section describes the impact of COVID-19 on higher education and the work that institutions face in the wake of the pandemic. We begin by describing the lessons that educational institutions learned during the pandemic in three contexts, following (openIDEO, 2020): remote learning, equity, and community. This section concludes with a discussion on certain insights about how design thinking can help universities to evolve.

3.4.1 Remote Learning

During the period of university closures, higher education institutions executed digital solutions (Wasik, 2020). At present, remote learning represents an opportunity for such institutions to offer greater flexibility to both students and instructors (Tarrayo et al., 2023). Hybrid and blended programs allow students and instructors to engage in the combined use of in-person and online learning (Zipper, 2022).

Undoubtedly, certain positive experiences emerged from the reactions of educational institutions, faculty, and students to the urgent situation that we all faced in 2020. Many educators learned what worked in the context of remote instruction and continue to be willing to employ these methods and practices and even combine them with face-to-face designs (Kim, 2021). Some educators, when forced to move online, seized the opportunity to innovate (Stevens et al., 2023). For example, some educators moved toward flipped designs to allow students to have their first encounter with the material through videos that they watched on their own and subsequently to come to class (which was conducted online during the pandemic) to work collaboratively. One aspect of remote learning that is highly valued by educators is the possibility of receiving real-time feedback from students (Baxter & Hainey, 2023). As noted in the Economist Intelligence Unit (EIU) report "Bridging the Digital Divide to Engage Students in Higher Education," which was sponsored by Microsoft Higher Education, 86% of faculty are convinced the use of tools to offer personalized, real-time feedback and flexible assessment will continue in the long term (Wasik, 2020).

For students, the pandemic experience was often complicated and frustrating, but it demonstrated their capacity to assert ownership over their own learning. Additionally, it forced them to analyze their own learning: the manner in which they learn, what they like, and what support they need (Anderson, 2020). The rapid shift to online teaching introduced flexibility into the learning process. This element improved students' learning experiences, and they discovered that they could personalize their learning due to the emergence of more customized environments.

However, one main truth that institutions and faculty discovered in this context is that, beyond this initial success, future online teaching and learning must be more than what many professors did and many students experienced during the pandemic; merely broadcasting videoconferences—a strategy on which many educators relied—is not sufficient (Zipper, 2022). This conclusion pertains not only to educational institutions but also to companies, industries, and public administrations, which must design better support for lifelong learning and the development of a generation of talent that is prepared for the challenges of tomorrow (IDEO, 2022b). Zipper (2022) summarizes these intuitions, concluding that the future avoids the dilemma of "online vs. classroom learning," substituting it for a unified format (hybrid or blended) that looks for quality and aims to provide high-impact learning regardless of the modality.

In this sense, the main lesson learned from the pandemic is that higher education institutions will invest in a blended future that features hybrid learning (Wasik, 2020). If educators want to maintain student engagement, it is necessary to make both traditional classrooms and virtual classrooms more engaging and personalized based on student-centered learning experiences and the use of new technologies to ensure active learning (Curtin, 2021; Wasik, 2020). This challenge elicits increased creativity and innovation from educators at all levels, who are rethinking their practices, developing new solutions, and reimagining learning experiences (Kim, 2021).

3.4.2 Equity in Education

During the pandemic, educational institutions, administrators, and policymakers realized that educational systems exhibit more disparities and inequalities than were before (Wasik, 2020). The transition to remote learning showed that, for many students and some educators, education was not as accessible as it was supposed to be (Bećirović & Dervić, 2023). The full extent of the digital divide became obvious, and instead of shrinking, it has continued to widen (Curtin, 2021).

Undoubtedly, higher education in the wake of COVID-19 should become more accessible and inclusive. Thus, the main lesson learned in this context is that educational systems should be reimagined to make learning more accessible. Equitable learning outcomes demand a systems-level redesign facilitated by collaboration among different partners and stakeholders (Curtin, 2021).

3.4.3 Community Building

The overnight transition to remote learning, including all the possibilities this shift opened up, is impressive. Nevertheless, it is also clear that remote learning will not replace the campus experience for the majority of faculty and students (Buckley et al., 2023). The sense of belonging to a community has an enormous effect on students' engagement and is an essential determinant of their success. This claim is especially true in the context of higher education, and this element suffered the most during the pandemic. Due to the fact that their learning communities grew weaker due to 100% online teaching, students faced difficulties keeping up academically (Curtin, 2021).

The main lesson learned in this context is that higher education institutions must evolve to take advantage of instructional and technological solutions that simultaneously offer flexibility and promote relationships both among students and between students and teachers (Tang et al., 2023). The potential of remote modalities (as well as on-campus modalities) can be achieved through active learning experiences that highlight the social nature of learning (Anderson, 2020).

3.4.4 Design Thinking as a Tool for the Future

Based on these lessons, the challenges faced by institutions of higher education are clear: they should not only promote hybrid learning models and increase their investments in technology but also involve administrators, staff, faculty, students, and other stakeholders in designing the active, inclusive, and social learning that the future demands (Wasik, 2020).

This point is where design thinking can play a substantial role. Designers and experts from IDEO are convinced that design thinking could help institutions of higher education face the challenges of education in the wake of COVID-19. To open this debate at the most critical moment of the crisis, in June 2020, IDEO organized a webinar to discuss ways of rethinking learning beyond the pandemic (openIDEO, 2020). The proposed design challenge was as follows: "How might we help educators, parents, and students adapt to remote learning while also using this moment to radically reimagine what we need our education systems to be?" (openIDEO, 2020). IDEO collected contributions from around the world that addressed the three challenges outlined earlier: remote learning, equity, and community.

As experts realized that design thinking can be useful for the task of reimagining education, the challenge evolved, and in 2022, IDEO proposed a new question: "How can design advance learning and education?" (IDEO, 2022b). One proposal for incorporating design thinking into higher education emerges from Bowdoin College (Maine, the United States). The project "Rethinking College Admissions" (Bowdoin College, 2022) aims to redesign the Bowdoin admissions department to help staff meet growing demand by developing a more efficient and inclusive way of reading applications.

We have shown how institutions of higher education can and do use design thinking both to improve classroom experiences and to solve institutional problems. A broader adoption of design thinking in higher education could help administrators, staff, faculty, and students address, in an innovative way, the difficulties that will be faced by higher education in the future, which will never be the same in the wake of COVID-19. Nevertheless, in the various sections of this chapter, we highlighted several problems and difficulties that are inherent to the task of developing a design thinking process: the challenge of ensuring that staff, students, and administrators are involved in the process; the provision of the training necessary to be able to participate in the process; the time and extra work demanded by the task of applying these processes in the classroom; and the change in mentality that this process implies. A possible way of addressing these drawbacks and ensuring success with respect to this innovative way of finding solutions is to introduce gamification elements into the design thinking process. The following chapter is devoted to the incorporation of gamification and design thinking into higher education.

References

Ahmadi, R., & Hasani, M. (2018). Capturing student voice on TEFL syllabus design: Agenticity of pedagogical dialogue negotiation. *Cogent Education, 5*(1), 1522780.

Anderson, J. (2020). How coronavirus is changing education. *Quartz*. Retrieved from https://qz.com/1826369/how-coronavirus-is-changing-education/

Bahou, L. (2011). Rethinking the challenges and possibilities of student voice and agency. *Educate, 1*(1), 2–14.

Bakırlıoğlu, Y. (2023). *Roles and capabilities of stakeholders in open design-driven distributed value creation for localised circular economies*. Cleaner Environmental Systems. *10*, 100129.

Baroutsis, A., McGregor, G., & Mills, M. (2016). Pedagogic voice: Student voice in teaching and engagement pedagogies. *Pedagogy, Culture & Society, 24*(1), 123–140.

Baxter, G., & Hainey, T. (2023). Remote learning in the context of COVID-19: Reviewing the effectiveness of synchronous online delivery. *Journal of Research in Innovative Teaching & Learning, 16*(1), 67–81.

Bećirović, S., & Dervić, M. (2023). Students' perspectives of digital transformation of higher education in Bosnia and Herzegovina. *The Electronic Journal of Information Systems in Developing Countries, 89*(2), e12243.

Bertão, R. A., Jung, C. H., Chung, J., & Joo, J. (2023). Design thinking: A customized blueprint to train R & D personnel in creative problem-solving. *Thinking Skills and Creativity, 48*, 101253.

Binkley, M., Erstad, O., Herman, J., Raizen, S., Ripley, M., Miller-Ricci, M., & Rumble, M. (2012). Defining twenty-first century skills. In P. Griffin, B. Mcgaw, & E. Care (Eds.), *Assessment and teaching of 21st century skills* (pp. 17–66). Dordrecht: Springer.

Bizami, N. A., Tasir, Z., & Kew, S. N. (2023). Innovative pedagogical principles and technological tools capabilities for immersive blended learning: A systematic literature review. *Education and Information Technologies, 28*(2), 1373–1425.

Blair, E., & Valdez Noel, K. (2014). Improving higher education practice through student evaluation systems: Is the student voice being heard? *Assessment & Evaluation in Higher Education, 39*(7), 879–894.

Bonwell, C. C., & Eison, J. A. (1991). *Active learning: Creating excitement in the classroom* (1991 ASHE-ERIC Higher Education Reports). ERIC Clearinghouse on Higher Education, The George Washington University, One Dupont Circle, Suite 630, Washington, DC 20036-1183.

Boonkhum, P. (2023). Application of design thinking to the organization's policy and plan department. *International Journal of Sociologies and Anthropologies Science Reviews*, 3(1), 93–102.

Bowdoin College. (2022). Rethinking college admissions. *ideo.com*. Retrieved from www.ideo.com/case-study/rethinking-college-admissions

Bowen, J. A. (2012). *Teaching naked: How moving technology out of your college classroom will improve student learning*. San Francisco, CA: John Wiley & Sons.

Buckley, J. B., Robinson, B. S., Tretter, T. R., Biesecker, C., Hammond, A. N., & Thompson, A. K. (2023). Belonging as a gateway for learning: First-year engineering students' characterizations of factors that promote and detract from sense of belonging in a pandemic. *Journal of Engineering Education*, *112*, 816–839.

Calavia, M. B., Blanco, T., Casas, R., & Dieste, B. (2023). Making design thinking for education sustainable: Training preservice teachers to address practice challenges. *Thinking Skills and Creativity*, *47*, 101199.

CAST. (2022). About universal design for learning. *CAST*. Retrieved from www.cast.org/impact/universal-design-for-learning-udl

CEDEFOP. (2022). Skills in online job advertisements. *CEDEFOP*. Retrieved from www.cedefop.europa.eu/en/tools/skills-intelligence/skills-online-job-advertisements?year=2021&occupation=&country=EU27_2020#1

Center for Curriculum Redesign. (2022). Retrieved from https://curriculumredesign.org/

Council of the European Union (2009). Council conclusions of 12 May 2009 on a strategic framework for European cooperation in education and training ('ET 2020'). *Official Journal of the European Union*, C 119/2, 28.5.2009.

Curtin, R. (2021). Reimagining higher education: The post-covid classroom. *EDUCAUSE*. Retrieved from https://er.educause.edu/articles/2021/4/reimagining-higher-education-the-post-covid-classroom

Datar, S. (2022). Design thinking course. *HBS Online*. Retrieved from https://online.hbs.edu/courses/design-thinking-innovation/

Dilekçi, A., & Karatay, H. (2023). The effects of the 21st century skills curriculum on the development of students' creative thinking skills. *Thinking Skills and Creativity*, *47*, 101229.

Dweck, C. S. (2006). *Mindset: The new psychology of success*. Random House.

Dym, C. L., Agogino, A. M., Eris, O., Frey, D. D., & Leifer, L. J. (2005). Engineering design thinking, teaching, and learning. *Journal of Engineering Education*, 94(1), 103–120.

Educate! Experience (2020). *OpenIDEO—Idea: Delivering remote educational engagement and skills training to youth*. Retrieved from https://challenges.openideo.com/challenge/covid-19-reimagine-learning-challenge/idea/delivering-remote-educational-engagementand-skills-training-to-youth?documentId=8dd79f8bb645b25821ffe83ca52bbf70&documentTableId=1297037795598995862

Efeoğlu, A., & Møller, C. (2023). Redesigning design thinking for codesign with non-designers: A method efficiency perspective. *Design Science*, *9*, e14.

Ellem, J. (2018). Design thinking is the driver. *STEM Education Conference 2018*, Deakin University, Geelong Waurn Ponds Campus, 11 November 2018. Retrieved from www.deakin.edu.au/__data/assets/pdf_file/0009/1853253/Design-Thinking-as-the-Driver.pdf

European Commission. (2018, January 17). Commission staff working document accompanying the document Proposal for a Council Recommendation on Key Competences for Lifelong Learning. COM (2018) 24 final, Brussels. Retrieved from https://eur-lex.europa.eu/legal-content/EN/TXT/PDF/?uri=CELEX:52018SC0014&from=EN

European Commission. (2022). Commission staff working document accompanying the document Proposal for a Council Recommendation on Key Competences for Lifelong Learning. COM (2018) 24 final, Brussels, January 17. Retrieved from https://eur-lex.europa.eu/legal-content/EN/TXT/PDF/?uri=CELEX:52018SC0014&from=EN

Felder, M., Kleinhout-Vliek, T., Stevens, M., & de Bont, A. (2023). From 'if only' to 'what if': An ethnographic study into design thinking and organizational change. *Design Studies*, *86*, 101178.

Fink, L. D. (2013). *Creating significant learning experiences: An integrated approach to designing college courses*. San Framcisco, CA: John Wiley & Sons.

Flipped Learning Network (FLN). (2014). The four pillars of FLIP™. Flipped Learning Network. Pennsylvania, US. Retrieved from http://www.flippedlearning.org/definition

Fortune, J., Burke, J., Dillon, C., Dillon, S., O'Toole, S., Enright, A., . . . Ryan, J. M. (2022). Co-designing resources to support the transition from child to adult health services for young people with cerebral palsy: A design thinking approach. *Frontiers in Rehabilitation Sciences*, *3*, 976580.

Gaebel, M., Zhang, T., Bunescu, L., & Stoeber, H. (2018). *Learning and teaching in the European higher education area*. European University Association asbl, Brussels, Belgium.

Gasca, J. (2015). Design thinking. Afrontar los retos con la actitud de un diseñador. *Leaners Magazine*, *8*, 22–25.

Ghannam, R., & Chan, C. (2023). Teaching undergraduate students to think like real-world systems engineers: A technology-based hybrid learning approach. *Systems Engineering*, 1–14.

Guaman-Quintanilla, S., Chiluiza, K., Everaert, P., & Valcke, M. (2018). Design thinking in higher education: A scoping review. In *11th annual international conference of education, research and innovation (ICERI)* (pp. 2954–2963). International Academy of Technology, Education and Development (IATED). Seville, Spain.

Guaman-Quintanilla, S., Everaert, P., Chiluiza, K., & Valcke, M. (2022). Impact of design thinking in higher education: A multi-actor perspective on problem solving and creativity. *International Journal of Technology and Design Education*, *24*. doi:10.1007/s10798-021-09724-z

Hamlin, J., & Janssen, S. (1987). Active learning in large introductory sociology courses. *Teaching Sociology*, 45–54.

Han, E. (2022). What is design thinking & why is it important? *HBS Online*. Retrieved from https://online.hbs.edu/blog/post/what-is-design-thinking#:~:text=Design%20thinking%20is%20an%20extension,mastered%20through%20practice%20with%20peers

Hasso Plattner Institute of Design at Stanford University (2023). d.School, Archival Resource, *Design Thinking Bootcamp Bootleg*. Available online: https://dschool.stanford.edu/resources/the-bootcamp-bootleg (accessed on 13 October 2023).

IDEO. (2022a). About IDEO: Our story, who we are, how we work. *ideo.com*. Retrieved from www.ideo.com/about

IDEO. (2022b). How can design advance learning and education? *ideo.com*. Retrieved from www.ideo.com/question/how-can-design-advance-education

Jiang, C., & Pang, Y. (2023). Enhancing design thinking in engineering students with project-based learning. *Computer Applications in Engineering Education, 31*, 814–830.

Katsumata Shah, M., Jactat, B., Yasui, T., & Ismailov, M. (2023). Low-fidelity prototyping with design thinking in higher education management in Japan: Impact on the utility and usability of a student exchange program brochure. *Education Sciences, 13*(1), 53.

Kaygan, P. (2023). From forming to performing: Team development for enhancing interdisciplinary collaboration between design and engineering students using design thinking. *International Journal of Technology and Design Education, 33*(2), 457–478.

Kelley, T., & Kelley, D. (2013). *Creative confidence: Unleashing the creative potential within us all*. Currency. New York, US.

Kennedy, J., & Pek, S. (2023). Mini-publics, student participation, and universities' deliberative capacity. *Studies in Higher Education, 48*(1), 63–82.

Kerr, N. L., & Tindale, R. S. (2004). Group performance and decision making. *Annual Review of Psychology, 55*(1), 623–655.

Kim, H. J., Yi, P., & Ko, B. W. (2023). Deepening students' experiences with problem identification and definition in an empathetic approach: Lessons from a university design-thinking program. *Journal of Applied Research in Higher Education, 15*(3), 852–865.

Kim, J. (2021). Universal design for learning after COVID-19. *Learning Innovation*. Retrieved from www.insidehighered.com/blogs/learning-innovation/universal-design-learning-after-covid-19

Kolodner, J. L., & Wills, L. M. (1996). Powers of observation in creative design. *Design Studies, 17*(4), 385–416.

Krolikowski, K. A., Bi, M., Baggott, C. M., Khorzad, R., Holl, J. L., & Kruser, J. M. (2022). Design thinking to improve healthcare delivery in the intensive care unit: Promise, pitfalls, and lessons learned. *Journal of Critical Care, 69*, 153999.

Kurek, J., Brandli, L. L., Leite Frandoloso, M. A., Lange Salvia, A., & Mazutti, J. (2023). Sustainable business models innovation and design thinking: A bibliometric analysis and systematic review of literature. *Sustainability, 15*(2), 988.

Latorre-Cosculluela, C., Vázquez-Toledo, S., Rodríguez-Martínez, A., & Liesa-Orús, M. (2020). Design thinking: Creatividad y pensamiento crítico en la universidad. *Revista Electrónica de Investigación Educativa, 22*. https://doi.org/10.24320/redie.2020.22.e28.2917

Laundry, L. (2020). What is human-centered design? *HBS Online*. Retrieved from https://online.hbs.edu/blog/post/what-is-human-centered-design

Lee, J. S., Blackwell, S., Drake, J., & Moran, K. A. (2014). Taking a leap of faith: Redefining teaching and learning in higher education through project-based learning. *Interdisciplinary Journal of Problem-Based Learning, 8*(2), 2.

Lemke, C. (2002). *enGauge 21st century skills: Digital literacies for a digital age*. Retrieved from https://eric.ed.gov/?id=ED463753

Lemström, T. (2023). What is the importance of design thinking for future healthcare? In *Design thinking in healthcare: From problem to innovative solutions* (pp. 113–119). Cham: Springer International Publishing.

Leonard, S. N., Fitzgerald, R. N., & Riordan, G. (2016). Using developmental evaluation as a design thinking tool for curriculum innovation in professional higher

education. *Higher Education Research & Development, 35*(2), 309–321. doi:10.108
0/07294360.2015.1087386
Lin, M. F. G., & Eichelberger, A. (2020). Design thinking as a catalyst for change: Faculty reaction to a redesigned meeting. *Journal of Formative Design in Learning, 4*(1), 34–42. doi:10.1007/s41686-020-00046-2
Lo Presti, O., & Carli, M. R. (2023). Promoting underground cultural heritage through sustainable practices: A design thinking and audience development approach. *Sustainability, 15*(11), 9125.
Luka, I. (2019). Design thinking in pedagogy: Frameworks and uses. *European Journal of Education, 54*(4), 499–512. doi:10.1111/ejed.12367
Mann, C. (2020). Advising by design: Co-creating advising services with students for their success. *Frontiers in Education, 5*, 9. doi:10.3389/feduc.2020.00099
Matthews, J., & Wrigley, C. (2017). Design and design thinking in business and management higher education. *Journal of Learning Design, 10*(1), 41–54.
Matthews, K. E., & Dollinger, M. (2023). Student voice in higher education: The importance of distinguishing student representation and student partnership. *Higher Education, 85*(3), 555–570.
Micheli, P., Wilner, S. J., Bhatti, S. H., Mura, M., & Beverland, M. B. (2019). Doing design thinking: Conceptual review, synthesis, and research agenda. *Journal of Product Innovation Management, 36*(2), 124–148.
McLaughlan, R., & Lodge, J. M. (2019). Facilitating epistemic fluency through design thinking: A strategy for the broader application of studio pedagogy within higher education. *Teaching in Higher Education, 24*(1), 81–97. doi:10.1080/13562517.20 18.1461621
Moretti, D. M., Baum, C. M., Wustmans, M., & Bröring, S. (2022). Application of journey maps to the development of emergent sustainability-oriented technologies: Lessons for user involvement in agriculture. *Business Strategy & Development, 5*(3), 209–221.
Nicolai, M., & Thompson, N. A. (2023). 'How might we?': Studying new venture ideation in and through practices. *Scandinavian Journal of Management, 39*(2), 101275.
Norman, D. A., & Spohrer, J. C. (1996). Learner-centered education. *Communications of the ACM, 39*(4), 24–27.
openIDEO. (2020). COVID-19 reimagine learning challenge. *OpenIDEO*. Retrieved from www.openideo.com/challenge-briefs/covid-19-reimagine-learning-challenge
Plattner, H., Meinel, C., & Leifer, L. (2012). *Design thinking research*. Cham, Switzerland: Springer.
Pope-Ruark, R., Moses, J., & Tham, J. (2019). Iterating the literature: An early annotated bibliography of design-thinking resources. *Journal of Business and Technical Communication, 33*(4), 456–465. doi:10.1177/1050651919854096
Razzouk, R., & Shute, V. (2012). What is design thinking and why is it important? *Review of Educational Research, 82*(3), 330–348.
Robinson, K. (2016). Do schools kill creativity? *TED Talk*. Retrieved from www.ted.com/talks/sir_ken_robinson_do_schools_kill_creativity?language=es
Rösch, N., Tiberius, V., & Kraus, S. (2023). Design thinking for innovation: Context factors, process, and outcomes. *European Journal of Innovation Management, 26*(7), 160–176.
Santos Ordóñez, A., Gonzalez Lema, C., Miño Puga, M. F., Párraga Lema, C., & Calderon Vega, F. (2017). *Design thinking as a methodology for solving problems: Contributions from academia to society*. Paper presented at the Global Partnerships for

Development and Engineering Education: Proceedings of the 15th LACCEI International Multi-Conference for Engineering, Education and Technology.

Scheer, A., Noweski, C., & Meinel, C. (2012). Transforming constructivist learning into action: Design thinking in education. *Design and Technology Education: An International Journal, 17*(3).

Selamet, J. (2023). Applying health design thinking to uncover actors in the sustenance of health and wellbeing during hotel quarantine in Kuwait. *Visual Communication, 22*(1), 202–217.

Southworth, J., Migliaccio, K., Glover, J., Reed, D., McCarty, C., Brendemuhl, J., & Thomas, A. (2023). Developing a model for AI across the curriculum: Transforming the higher education landscape via innovation in AI literacy. *Computers and Education: Artificial Intelligence, 4*, 100127.

Stevens, T. M., den Brok, P. J., Noroozi, O., & Biemans, H. J. A. (2023). Teacher profiles in higher education: The move to online education during the COVID-19 crisis. *Learning Environments Research, 26*, 873–898.

Tang, C., Thyer, L., Bye, R., Kenny, B., Tulliani, N., Peel, N., . . . Dark, L. (2023). Impact of online learning on sense of belonging among first year clinical health students during COVID-19: Student and academic perspectives. *BMC Medical Education, 23*, 100.

Tarrayo, V. N., Paz, R. M. O., & Gepila, E. C., Jr. (2023). The shift to flexible learning amidst the pandemic: The case of English language teachers in a Philippine state university. *Innovation in Language Learning and Teaching, 17*(1), 130–143.

Tschepe, S. (2018). How design thinking can benefit education. *The Startup | Medium*. Retrieved from https://medium.com/swlh/how-design-thinking-can-benefit-education-2bba35450771

Ungarean, M., Bixler, K., & Desmore, K. (2023). Forming a unique partnership between a university's educational leadership master's degree program and its surrounding school districts using the five whys protocol. *Journal of Formative Design in Learning, 7*, 17–26.

Vendraminelli, L., Macchion, L., Nosella, A., & Vinelli, A. (2023). Design thinking: Strategy for digital transformation. *Journal of Business Strategy, 44*(4), 200–210.

Verganti, R. (2009). *Design driven innovation: Changing the rules of competition by radically innovating what things mean*. Boston, Massachusetts, US: Harvard Business Press.

Wasik, E. (2020). *Bridging the digital divide to engage students in higher education*. Retrieved from https://impact.economist.com/perspectives/technology-innovation/bridging-digital-divide-engage-students-higher-education

Weimer, M. (2002). *Learner-centered teaching: five key changes to practice*. San Francisco, CA: Jossey Bass.

World Design Summit. (2017). *Montreal design declaration 2017*. Montreal, Canada. Retrieved from www.designdeclaration.org/wp-content/uploads/2019/01/Montreal_Design_Declaration_2017_WEB.pdf

World Economic Forum (2020). *The future of jobs report 2020*. Retrieved from https://www.weforum.org/reports/the-future-of-jobs-report-2020/in-full/infographics-e4e69e4de7

Zhang, X., Zhang, B., & Zhang, F. (2023). Student-centered case-based teaching and online–offline case discussion in postgraduate courses of computer science. *International Journal of Educational Technology in Higher Education, 20*(1), 6.

Zipper, T. (2022). *The future of online education in the wake of COVID-19*. Wiley. Retrieved from https://universityservices.wiley.com/future-of-online-education-in-the-wake-of-covid19/

4 Gamification and Design Thinking Applications in Higher Education

4.1 Introduction

After analyzing gamification and design thinking in-depth in the second and third chapters of this book, this chapter is dedicated to the combination of both factors. This chapter is structured as follows. First, we examine the ways in which these two techniques can be combined on the basis of a review of the literature. Subsequently, we discuss the ways in which the design thinking activities developed in the context of higher education can be gamified. We take the three steps discussed in Section 2.3 and adapt them to the context of design thinking.

Finally, we modify the two examples of activities based on design thinking in higher education that were explained in Chapter 3, that is, "What can this international organization do for you?" and "Our School would be much better if . . ." by adding a gamified design. In this way, we present in a practical way two proposals for activities in the field of higher education that combine gamification and design thinking. Our goal is to help the readers of the book understand this process and to inspire them through our examples.

4.2 Gamification and Design Thinking in the Literature

The literature contains few examples of the combination of gamification and design thinking, and those examples that can be found are focused on the business environment and the area of innovation (Patrício et al., 2020; Picanço & dos Santos, 2022) as well as the health sector (Korn et al., 2018). Accordingly, the literature contains few references to the joint application of gamification and design thinking in the framework of higher education (Hung, 2018).

Patrício et al. (2020) employ the case study methodology to explore the relationship between gamification and design thinking. For this purpose, these authors select three companies with different levels of experience, that is, Trivalor, Novartis, and Microsoft. The authors then introduce gamification during a specific phase of the design thinking process: the ideation phase. Instead of creating a gamified design, they use the ideaChef tool. ideaChef allows

DOI: 10.4324/9781032675558-4

groups of four to six individuals to propose ideas in a gamified environment. Patrício et al. (2020) conclude that gamification in this context helps provide clarity to participants regarding the objectives pursued through the specific design thinking activity and promotes their engagement. It also encourages more individuals to participate in this process, even those who find traditional design thinking methods to be boring, and it allows more disruptive ideas to be proposed. This approach thus improves the design thinking process, ultimately promoting innovation.

Hung (2018) details his combination of gamification and design thinking in a Philosophy of Technology course developed for a program in educational technology in higher education. This course is a blended course in which some classes are taught face to face and other classes are taught virtually. Hung (2018) employs only the learning management system used in his institution, Moodle, to develop a gamified design thinking activity. The goal of introducing gamified design thinking is to improve the students' experience in a course that may be complicated. Kessing and Löwer (2021) also propose the use of gamification to motivate participants to engage in design thinking in the university environment. However, these authors do not discuss how this combination can be implemented. Finally, Villegas et al. (2019) compare gamification and design thinking to identify the similarities and differences between the two approaches. These authors find that both methods give designers the freedom to adapt the method to the specific characteristics of the situation in which they are to be applied. These authors also note that both gamification and design thinking take individuals into account, positioning them at the center of the process, and in both cases they analyze the characteristics of users.

According to the explanations contained in this section, it is clear that the literature contains few references to the combination of gamification and design thinking and that, moreover, no guide is available to help us develop experiences that combine these two techniques. Therefore, we explain in the following that these techniques can be combined in the context of higher education.

4.3 How to Gamify an Activity Based on Design Thinking in Higher Education

Recall the explanation contained in Section 2.3. We noted that to gamify, a three-step process (Cechetti et al., 2019; De la Peña et al., 2021; Deterding, 2015) must be considered: (i) analysis (Cechetti et al., 2019), (ii) design and development (De la Peña et al., 2021), and (iii) implementation and evaluation (Deterding, 2015).

To gamify an activity based on a design thinking process developed in the context of higher education, we must follow the same steps. First, we analyze the manner in which the activity is to be gamified as well as its context, we determine the objectives that we are pursuing through gamification, and we analyze the nature of future participants.

With regard to the activity and its context, we must take into account its duration, the educational objective toward which it is directed, the size of the group involved, and whether it will be implemented in person or virtually, among other factors. Subsequently, we must determine what we intend to achieve through gamification. In the context of higher education, gamification is usually aimed at motivating and engaging students (Bouchrika et al., 2021; Zainuddin et al., 2020). These same objectives can be applied to a specific activity based on design thinking, although in our examples, our specific pursuit is to motivate students and encourage their engagement and participation.

Finally, we analyze the future participants and their behavior. This analysis is conducted in a general way in Subsection 2.1.3.1. At this point, we can complete this study and examine other traits, such as participants' personality and gender, as some studies indicate that the effects of gamification may vary on the basis of these factors (e.g., Denden et al., 2021; Pakinee & Puritat, 2021).

After the analysis step comes the design and development of the gamified experience. We start by studying the ways in which gamification has been applied to similar activities. Since the literature pertaining to gamification and design thinking in higher education is limited, we can investigate whether gamified experiences have been developed that exhibit other similarities with our activity, for example, experiences that also include the flipped classroom methodology (Murillo-Zamorano et al., 2019; Sailer & Sailer, 2021; Jia et al., 2023) or the use of augmented reality (Lampropoulos et al., 2022; Petrovych et al., 2023).

On the basis of all this information, we proceed to make decisions regarding the design of the activity in the subphase of its conception and construction. We discuss the necessary materials—slides, texts, videos, and so forth—and proceed to develop the design. This design is conditioned by the characteristics of the design thinking process. In Chapter 3, we commented that this design thinking process is composed of five phases: empathize, define, ideate, prototype, and evaluate. Therefore, our gamified design must adapt to these five phases.

We can ensure that the whole experience has a gamified design or apply this design merely to one or several of its phases. Gamifying the experience as a whole gives it meaning and makes it easier for learners to become engaged with it. We can also gamify merely one or several phases to encourage learner participation at particular points in the process. The design possibilities of gamification are very broad, and the designer of the experience must decide how to implement this approach.

Nevertheless, we must bear in mind that if the five phases of the design thinking process take place on different days, it is advisable to create mechanisms that encourage students to attend all sessions of the activity. If a student fails to attend a class, the student may feel lost during the following session and not be able to manage. To avoid this scenario, we can design a system that rewards attendance, which can be based on different elements that allow us to quantify progress and performance, such as points or badges.

In other words, in addition to defining the duration of the gamification process—whether it applies to one phase of the design thinking process, to several or to its entirety—we must also define the elements that we intend to introduce as well as in what way and at what time we intend to introduce them. As for the gamification elements to be introduced in our two examples, we are inspired by the taxonomy proposed by Toda et al. (2019) for gamification in educational environments. The taxonomy developed by Toda et al. (2019) comprises five dimensions: performance/measurement, ecological, social, personal, and fictional.

We also must decide whether we intend to introduce elements that act as rewards, measure performance, or confer meaning on the experience, among other decisions. In addition, we must decide the specific elements to include and how those elements should be structured.

In this step, we must consider whether we intend to opt for a design that encourages collaboration, competition, or a combination of both approaches. We can also choose to focus on coopetition. Coopetition refers to a combination of competition and cooperation. This term was coined in 1992 by Ray Norda, chief-executive officer (CEO) of the Novell company, to describe a phenomenon in the computer industry, which was characterized by cooperation between competitors (Dowling, 2020).

More recently, the term *coopetition* has been extended to many contexts. When applied to activities involving individuals and those that take place outside the context of industry, it refers to the creation of an environment of interdependence within a competitive context. Achievements are made with the support of the crowd, and participation takes place both individually and collectively. In this manner, an atmosphere of exchange and evaluation among members emerges (Renard & Davis, 2019; Murillo-Zamorano et al., 2020). Finally, we must decide whether we intend to resort to particular platforms to introduce gamification and, if so, which platforms are to be used.

The final step of the gamification process is the implementation and evaluation step. In this context, we implement the gamified design thinking activity with the participation of university students, monitoring its correct functioning and evaluating the results obtained through this process to make improvements in the future. It is also advisable to conduct a pilot test beforehand to verify the viability of the process.

4.4 Examples

In this section, we explain how gamification and design thinking can be combined through the redesign of the two design thinking examples described in the previous Chapter 3, namely "Example 1: What can this international organization do for you?" and "Example 2: Our school would be much better if. . .. " As described in Chapter 3, both design thinking examples followed the Stanford d.school model and employed a flipped learning structure. In this section, and to accomplish the goal of introducing a gamified design in a design thinking activity, we apply the gamification phases described in Chapter 2 to the two design thinking examples described in Chapter 3.

4.4.1 Example 1: "What Can This International Organization Do for You?"

4.4.1.1 Analysis

This activity is implemented in the context of the "Economics of the European Union" module in a business and economics course. The general objective of this subject is to explore the economic and political logic associated with the European integration process, providing the student with a basic understanding of the institutional architecture, the current situation, and the problems of European economies in the early 21st century. The specific objective of the activity, that is, "What can this international organization do for you?" which is positioned at the end of the semester, is to make students aware of the impact that EU policies have on the social or economic environment in any context and to help them integrate their technical knowledge of EU into an understanding of the real-world worries of Europeans.

As discussed in the previous chapter, this experience employs a flipped classroom approach. That is, students engage in activities both inside and outside the classroom. The participants are students in a business and economics course at the University of Oviedo (Spain). These students belong to Generation Z. Therefore, we must bear in mind their preference for the use of technology in an educational environment. Finally, the objective of gamification in this context is to motivate these students and engage them in the activity. This approach promotes their participation and commitment, thus making the experience more enriching and facilitating their acquisition of knowledge. It is also an activity that features a high level of difficulty. Gamification can be useful to prevent students from becoming demotivated and deciding not to make an effort.

4.4.1.2 Design and Development

As mentioned at the beginning of this chapter, the literature contains some cases that combine gamification and design thinking. However, there are very few examples of this combination, and hardly any references are made to their combination in the context of higher education. For this reason, in this step of the gamification design process, we briefly analyze the ways in which this process has been applied in combination with another technique that also structures our activity: the flipped classroom methodology.

In Section 2.4, we discussed the combined use of gamification and the flipped classroom approach. We noted that, according to Ekici's review (2021), the most frequently used elements in this context are points, badges, and leaderboards. With regard to platforms, the most common platforms used to introduce gamification are learning management systems, such as Moodle and Blackboard, as well as educational platforms whose purpose is to administer quizzes, such as Kahoot.

This information can inspire us when designing and developing our activity. Similarly, Ekici (2021) concludes in his literature review that, in general, gamification improves students' motivation and academic performance in this specific context. In the following, we address the conception and construction of the activity, highlighting its duration, the gamification elements selected, and the use of platforms.

DURATION

The first question to ask with regard to the design pertains to the duration of the gamified experience. The activity "What can this international organization do for you?" which is based on design thinking, consists of 5 sessions with a duration of 1–1.5 hours each as well as an initial presentation session. If we recall what was explained in the section regarding how to gamify an educational activity as well as, more precisely, what was mentioned in the section pertaining to the duration of the activity, we can see that the impact of gamification follows a U-shaped curve (Rodrigues et al., 2022).

Specifically, the initial effects of gamification decrease over time (the novelty effect). This phenomenon occurs after four weeks of activity. Subsequently, the effects increase until they reach their initial levels (the familiarization effect). This effect occurs between the sixth and tenth week after the start of the activity (Rodrigues et al., 2022).

The activity "What can this international organization do for you?" consists of five sessions. If one session were conducted per week, the total duration of the educational activity would be five weeks. In this situation, in light of the effects mentioned earlier, we would run the risk of diminishing the influence exerted by gamification on student motivation. For this reason, it is more convenient to structure the activity in such a way that two sessions are conducted per week. In this way, we achieve a total duration of less than three weeks and thus take advantage of the novelty effect of gamification on student motivation (Kratochvil et al., 2023).

ELEMENTS

On the basis of the explanations contained in Chapter 2, we know that many gamification elements can be included in our design. In this case, the elements chosen are the following: narrative, collaboration, points, reputation, missions, time pressure, social pressure, and chat.

PLATFORM

The use of gamified platforms is optional. For this reason, for the purpose of demonstrating how we can gamify without using digital platforms, this activity will be carried out exclusively in person. For the other activity chosen as an example in this book, we will use such a platform. Thus, we present two alternatives that may be useful for teachers who are interested in these techniques regardless of whether they have access to digital platforms.

4.4.1.3 Implementation and Evaluation

In this step, the gamified design thinking activity is implemented. It is advisable to conduct a pilot test to evaluate the performance of the activity. The phases of our design thinking activity, "What can this international organization do for you?" as adapted through gamification are as follows.

Session 0 (Present): The initial session or session 0 consists of a one-hour presentation. In this presentation, the teacher explains to the students the project, its aims, the ways in which it will be carried out, and the manner in which it will be assessed. At this point, the first element of gamification present in our activity is introduced: the narrative. Specifically, we cause the students to feel as if they are stakeholders who will be influenced by the EU, and this narrative will guide the whole experience. The aim of this approach is to involve students in the activity. In addition, through this narrative, we also cause them to feel as if they are the protagonists of the activity. Moreover, the activity will be carried out in groups, which is another element of gamification and facilitates collaboration among participants. In this case, competition is not present since the groups will not compete with each other to win.

Subsequently, students define the audience by engaging in brainstorming to identify who constitutes the "you," that is, who are the stakeholders that are impacted by the EU (citizens, customers, firms, families, people of different ages, etc.). Some students may participate less fully in this process due to disinterest or embarrassment, among other reasons. To encourage their participation, we can use gamification and offer rewards. In our case, we will award one point for each proposal they make during the brainstorming process that is ultimately chosen. As mentioned, competition is not present in our experience. These points are not linked to competition. That is, we will not use a leaderboard to compare the points accumulated by each student. In contrast, the points assigned to the students generate reputation and status.

Finally, students must engage in an out-of-class activity based on the flipped classroom methodology that we employ. This activity consists of researching the stakeholders that they have been assigned.

Session 1 (Empathize): The first session, which lasts 1–1.5 hours, focuses on the empathize phase of the design thinking process. In this session, students share with their groups the knowledge that they obtained from the previous test using post-it notes. Following this step, they collaboratively develop an interview guide to obtain more information from the selected stakeholders. A role playing exercise is also conducted; half of the students in each group interview the other half, who play the role of the relevant stakeholder. As in the previous session, students are assigned an out-of-class activity. In this case, this activity requires them to attempt to interview a real-world stakeholder.

The objective of this session is to obtain as much information as possible to allow students to participate in the subsequent session (session 2: define). This process can be compared to a mission. Completing a mission can be used as a requirement to obtain badges (Jakubowski, 2014). Analogously, we will establish that completing the mission of obtaining sufficient information regarding the assigned stakeholder is a prerequisite to being able to access the subsequent session. That is, in our experience, we identify the completion of a mission as a requirement to access the next phase or level.

Session 2 (Define): The second session corresponds to the define phase and lasts one hour. As in the previous phase, students share the knowledge they acquired with the other members of their group by means of post-it notes. The aim of this session is to choose a specific challenge that is neither too narrow nor too broad, for which students will try to devise solutions in the subsequent session of the design thinking process (session 3: ideate). In this session, as in session 0, we will offer a reward to the students in each group who identify the best questions. Specifically, each group must develop a list of the five best options, based on which they must ultimately choose one of these five challenges. We will award one point to each student who proposes one of these five preselected challenges and another point to the author of the challenge that is ultimately chosen. Using this element—the points—we can motivate the students to improve their effort in accomplishing the task to achieve a better reputation.

The out-of-class activity that the students should perform between sessions consists of viewing a video outlining the following session. Individually, they research the laws, policies, budget, conditions, and so forth, associated with the EU that could affect the situation and complete a worksheet summarizing all their individual knowledge.

Session 3 (Ideate): The third session coincides with the third phase of the design thinking process, that is, the ideate stage, and is developed over the course of one hour. The prototype format proposed by the teacher in this session is the storyboard. During this phase, creativity takes precedence. For students to take advantage of their talents and develop original ideas, a climate of trust must be established in which they are not judged. Therefore, it is not advisable to introduce competitive social interactions in this context. In the previous sessions, the members of a group were required to identify the best proposals. In this session, on the other hand, students must cocreate the prototype and work collaboratively. In this session, we do not introduce any gamification element beyond the narrative and the collaboration (teams) that are present throughout the experience.

The out-of-class activity following session 3 consists of watching a video about storyboards. This video is necessary to enable the students to participate in session 4 (the prototype stage), in which they are required to develop a storyboard. Specifically, the video outlines the following session, the main elements of a storyboard, and the resources that are necessary to create a storyboard.

Session 4 (Prototype): The fourth session corresponds to the prototype phase and, like the previous sessions, has a duration of one hour. Students create the storyboard and prepare a poster explaining the challenge they intend to address (the concrete aspect of the problem on which they have decided to focus) as well as their proposed solution. This task is complex, as the students are unfamiliar with storyboards. Again, creativity takes precedence in this session, and we should not introduce elements that generate competition.

This step is the penultimate session, in which students must elaborate on the final product that they will present in the session with which this experience culminates. Therefore, we must establish a deadline, generating time pressure, to ensure that students complete the task on time. In addition, prior to the next session and outside the classroom, students must prepare for the final session, in which all groups must participate: each group will be assigned a specific stakeholder role to play as part of a role-playing exercise conducted during the final session. To prepare for the role-playing exercise, each design group will share with the stakeholder the notes regarding that concrete stakeholder type that they used to develop their solution. To guide them in this task, we will provide the students with a video outlining the subsequent session so that it is clear what they are expected to do.

Session 5 (Testing): The final session, session 5, coincides with the final phase of the design thinking process, that is, that of testing. This session lasts 1–1.5 hours. In our experience, the evaluation of the prototypes developed by each group is the responsibility of their peers. We provide the students with a rubric to facilitate the evaluation and ensure that they perform it based on relevant criteria.

Each group must present its solution to the rest of the class. At this point, another element of gamification is introduced: social pressure. Students are exposed to the comments and actions of their peers. This social pressure motivates students and is intended to positively influence the effort they invest into the task. Finally, after the evaluation, students must reflect on the knowledge they acquired from the activity "What can this international organization do for you?" and elaborate a SWOT in a collaborative manner. With regard to this final task, we introduce the notion of chat. That is, we ask the students to create the SWOT together with their initial groups using collaborative Google Docs. Google Docs offers a chat functionality. This function is very useful for coordinating group work in the context of remote work.

Finally, when the activity comes to an end, we must evaluate the results and consider the possibility of making modifications to improve the design.

4.4.2 Example 2: "Our School Would Be Much Better If . . ."

4.4.2.1 Analysis

The objective of the activity "Our school would be much better if . . .," which simulates a call made by the Dean's Office, is to answer the question "What could be improved in the School of Business and Economics?" (in terms of study space, collaboration space, timetables, vending machines, water fountains, etc.).

The activity is implemented in the context of the School of Business and Economics as a whole. Unlike the previous example, which was framed for a specific group of students, this activity simulates a call to the community that constitutes the school to improve the school's facilities and services. In this context, although in our hypothetical example, the Dean's Office has called for meetings among administrators, staff, faculty, and students to address this challenge, the analyzed case focuses on the participation of students using the design thinking methodology.

Giving students a voice and allowing them to participate by contributing ideas for improving the school can be a motivating factor in its own right. Through this activity, students can be empowered, and their opinions and thoughts are valued. However, the introduction of gamification in this context can, once again, promote their participation and facilitate their involvement. This design technique aims to improve their performance and engagement. The ultimate goal is for students to develop proposals that increase the well-being of the community and their day-to-day lives.

4.4.2.2 Design and Development

The first step in the design and development of the activity is to study the ways in which gamification has been applied to similar activities. In the previous example, we could examine experiences using gamification and flipped classrooms. In this activity, we also used the flipped classroom methodology. Therefore, the previous reflections discussed in the context of the gamified activity "What can this international organization do for you?" are also applicable to this example.

DURATION

Our hypothetical case entitled "Our school would be much better if . . ." is developed, as was the previous example, to include six sessions, that is, session 0 and five sessions that correspond to the five phases of the design thinking process. Let us assume that the meetings with the leader were to take place once per week. In this case, the duration of the activity would be six weeks. As we explained in the subsection on the duration of the activity in the section pertaining to how to gamify an educational activity, the initial effects of gamification decrease over time. These effects subsequently increase until they reach their initial levels (the familiarization effect). This phenomenon occurs between the sixth and tenth week following the start of the activity (Rodrigues et al., 2022).

Therefore, given that the duration of our activity is six weeks, we must bear in mind the fact that the motivation generated by gamification may decrease in the final sessions. To avoid this scenario, we can rely on elements that help maintain motivation, such as challenges (Yen et al., 2019). If we do not provide advance notice of the challenges, we could also introduce the element of novelty. The introduction of these elements is explained in further detail in the section on "implementation and evaluation."

ELEMENTS

The elements that we selected to create the gamified design of our activity "Our School would be much better if . . ." are as follows: collaboration, competition, challenges, points, leaderboards, novelty, missions, deadlines, badges, and reputation.

PLATFORM

This activity is developed using the Google Forms platform. However, Google Forms is not a gamified platform. Therefore, in addition to this platform, we will resort to another platform that is focused exclusively on this purpose: Kahoot. Kahoot is one of the main gamified educational platforms. Using Kahoot, quizzes can be created in a simple way. The teacher can pose the questions that he or she wants to ask and provide several possible answers. Students then compete using internet-enabled devices. Kahoot awards points if the correct answer is selected. The number of points thus awarded depends on the speed of the participants' responses. When the quiz comes to an end, the platform displays a leaderboard that ranks the learners based on the number of points they have scored.

4.4.2.3 Implementation and Evaluation

Session 0 (Presentation): The initial session or session 0 consists of the presentation of the activity "Our school would be much better if. . .. " The person in charge of the activity explains to the students the phases included in the process and the tasks that they must carry out. This experience, like the previous experience, also focuses on groups of students. Therefore, the element of collaboration is present. To influence student motivation, we will also include the element of competition. In this way, the activity becomes a competition. The winner will be the group that uses the design thinking process to elaborate the proposal that receives the most votes. This goal is communicated to the students in session 0 to encourage them to invest their effort in all the sessions of the activity.

The out-of-class activities associated with the flipped classroom methodology consist of viewing two short videos, one of which focuses on explaining the project, while the other to introduce students to the task of creating a Google Forms survey. The activity will be carried out using Google Forms. In other words, students must know how to use this resource to participate in the activity.

Session 1 (Empathize): The first session coincides with the empathize phase of the design thinking process. However, before beginning this session, we will dedicate the first ten minutes of the time provided to the task of administering a questionnaire via the Kahoot platform to explore the issues explained in the explanatory video regarding Google Forms to ensure that students have visualized and assimilated the relevant information. This questionnaire encompasses several elements of gamification: it represents a challenge, offers rewards in the form of points, and generates competition due to its effect on the final leaderboard. In addition, since we have not previously warned students about this test, we introduce the element of novelty.

Next, we continue by introducing the empathize phase. The groups participating in this activity engage in brainstorming to answer the question "What could be improved in the School of Business and Economics?". Thereafter, each group selects a topic and creates a survey using Google Forms to obtain the opinions of the other students regarding their proposal. The out-of-class activities in which students must engage after the session consist of distributing the questionnaire and viewing a video outlining the following session.

74 *Gamification and Design Thinking Applications*

Once again, we rely on gamification, in particular, by providing students with a mission. The mission requires them to try to obtain the highest volume of responses to their survey. We also set a deadline to complete this mission, which ends when session 2 (the define phase) begins. The objective of the gamified design of this out-of-class activity is to encourage participants to make an effort to distribute the surveys they create by themselves, since it is advisable to ensure that a large number of students complete this questionnaire to obtain results that reflect the thinking of the students at the school.

Session 2 (Define): In the first five minutes of this session, we reveal the group that is the winner of the previous mission. Continuing to employ the gamified design to generate reputation, we reward this group with a badge that qualifies them as the group that exhibited the best performance on the mission. Subsequently, we introduce the define phase of the design thinking process. Students analyze the survey results and propose potential solutions. As an out-of-class activity, students elaborate their personal reflections on the proposals and view a video explaining how to use a CANVAS model.

Session 3 (Ideate): Unlike in session 1, at the beginning of session 3, we do not administer a Kahoot questionnaire to verify that the students have watched the video regarding the CANVAS model and understood the information it contains. This approach is designed to ensure that the students do not become familiar with to the requirement of completing a questionnaire after viewing a video pertaining to the use of a new tool and to ensure that the novelty element can be reintroduced in the subsequent session. Session 3 coincides with the ideate phase. The groups select one of the proposals from the previous session and recreate it using the CANVAS model. At the end of the session, the students must watch a video regarding what a prototype is and how one can be created outside the classroom.

Session 4 (Prototype): As in session 2, we dedicate the first ten minutes of this session to a Kahoot quiz focused on the questions addressed in the explanatory video regarding what a prototype is and how one can be created. This approach ensures that the students have visualized and understood this information. Once again, gamification is used, particularly the following elements: challenge, points, leaderboard, and novelty. This quiz is followed by the prototype phase. In this phase, the students in each group discuss the type of prototype that is most suitable for the proposed solution and create such a prototype. The out-of-class activity that students must complete between this session and the final session consists of watching a video regarding the next session and reminding them how to create a SWOT.

Session 5 (Test): The final session is the testing phase. Each group presents its proposal, and the stakeholders vote on which idea is best. Voting takes place using Google Forms. In this case, the questionnaire is created by the person who is in charge of the activity. The group receiving the most votes is then announced as the winner of the contest, and a badge is awarded to this group to give them recognition and reputation. When the activity comes to an end, the participants reflect on the activity and what they have learned be engaging in it, and they analyze ways in which they can improve their proposals by elaborating a SWOT analysis as a group.

References

Bouchrika, I., Harrati, N., Wanick, V., & Wills, G. (2021). Exploring the impact of gamification on student engagement and involvement with e-learning systems. *Interactive Learning Environments, 29*(8), 1244–1257.

Cechetti, N. P., Bellei, E. A., Biduski, D., Rodriguez, J. P. M., Roman, M. K., & De Marchi, A. C. B. (2019). Developing and implementing a gamification method to improve user engagement: A case study with an m-Health application for hypertension monitoring. *Telematics and Informatics, 41*, 126–138.

de la Peña, D., Lizcano, D., & Martínez-Álvarez, I. (2021). Learning through play: Gamification model in university-level distance learning. *Entertainment Computing, 39*, 100430.

Denden, M., Tlili, A., Essalmi, F., Jemni, M., Chen, N. S., & Burgos, D. (2021). Effects of gender and personality differences on students' perception of game design elements in educational gamification. *International Journal of Human-Computer Studies, 154*, 102674.

Deterding, S. (2015). The lens of intrinsic skill atoms: A method for gameful design. *Human–Computer Interaction, 30*(3–4), 294–335.

Dowling, M. (2020). Coopetition. In *Oxford research encyclopedia of business and management*. Recuperado de. Retrieved from https://oxfordre.com/business/view/10.1093/acrefore/9780190224851.001.0001/acrefore-9780190224851-e-9

Ekici, M. (2021). A systematic review of the use of gamification in flipped learning. *Education and Information Technologies, 26*(3), 3327–3346.

Hung, A. C. Y. (2018). Gamification as design thinking. *International Journal of Teaching and Learning in Higher Education, 30*(3), 549–559.

Jakubowski, M. (2014, March). Gamification in business and education–project of gamified course for university students. In *Developments in business simulation and experiential learning: Proceedings of the annual ABSEL conference, 41*, 339–342.

Jia, C., Hew, K. F., Jiahui, D., & Liuyufeng, L. (2023). Towards a fully online flipped classroom model to support student learning outcomes and engagement: A 2-year design-based study. *The Internet and Higher Education, 56*, 100878.

Kessing, D., & Löwer, M. (2020, October). Work-in-progress: Gamification and design thinking–a motivational analysis of an international, interdisciplinary, team-based university course. In *International conference on interactive collaborative and blended learning* (pp. 65–73). Cham: Springer.

Korn, O., Buchweitz, L., Rees, A., Bieber, G., Werner, C., & Hauer, K. (2018, July). Using augmented reality and gamification to empower rehabilitation activities and elderly persons. A study applying design thinking. In *International conference on applied human factors and ergonomics* (pp. 219–229). Cham: Springer.

Kratochvil, T., Vaculik, M., & Macak, M. (2023, February). Gamification tailored for novelty effect in distance learning during COVID-19. In *Frontiers in education* (Vol. 8, p. 1051227). Laussane, Switzerland: Frontiers Media SA.ja

Lampropoulos, G., Keramopoulos, E., Diamantaras, K., & Evangelidis, G. (2022). Augmented reality and gamification in education: A systematic literature review of research, applications, and empirical studies. *Applied Sciences, 12*(13), 6809.

Murillo-Zamorano, L. R., López-Sánchez, J. A., & Bueno-Muñoz, C. (2020). Gamified crowdsourcing in higher education: A theoretical framework and a case study. *Thinking Skills and Creativity, 36*, 100645.

Murillo-Zamorano, L. R., López-Sánchez, J. A., & Godoy-Caballero, A. L. (2019). How the flipped classroom affects knowledge, skills, and engagement in higher education: Effects on students' satisfaction. *Computers & Education, 141*, 103608.

Pakinee, A., & Puritat, K. (2021). Designing a gamified e-learning environment for teaching undergraduate ERP course based on big five personality traits. *Education and Information Technologies, 26*, 4049–4067.

Patrício, R., Moreira, A. C., & Zurlo, F. (2020). Enhancing design thinking approaches to innovation through gamification. *European Journal of Innovation Management, 24*(5), 1569–1594.

Petrovych, O., Zavalniuk, I., Bohatko, V., Poliarush, N., & Petrovych, S. (2023). Motivational readiness of future teachers-philologists to use the gamification with elements of augmented reality in education. *International Journal of Emerging Technologies in Learning, 18*(3), 4–21.

Picanço, C. T., & dos Santos, S. C. (2022). Promoting collaboration and creativity in process improvement: A proposal based on design thinking and gamification. In *Proceedings of the 24th international conference on enterprise information systems (ICEIS 2022)* (pp. 418–429). Online Streaming. Setubal, Portugal: SCITEPRESS—Science and Technology Publications.

Renard, D., & Davis, J. G. (2019). Social interdependence on crowdsourcing platforms. *Journal of Business Research, 103*, 186–194.

Rodrigues, L., Pereira, F. D., Toda, A. M., Palomino, P. T., Pessoa, M., Carvalho, L. S. G., . . . Isotani, S. (2022). Gamification suffers from the novelty effect but benefits from the familiarization effect: Findings from a longitudinal study. *International Journal of Educational Technology in Higher Education, 19*, 13.

Sailer, M., & Sailer, M. (2021). Gamification of in-class activities in flipped classroom lectures. *British Journal of Educational Technology, 52*(1), 75–90.

Toda, A. M., Klock, A. C., Oliveira, W., Palomino, P. T., Rodrigues, L., Shi, L., . . . Cristea, A. I. (2019). Analysing gamification elements in educational environments using an existing gamification taxonomy. *Smart Learning Environments, 6*, 16.

Villegas, E., Labrador, E., Fonseca, D., Fernández-Guinea, S., & Moreira, F. (2019, July). Design thinking and gamification: User centered methodologies. In *International conference on human-computer interaction* (pp. 115–124). Cham: Springer.

Yen, B. T., Mulley, C., & Burke, M. (2019). Gamification in transport interventions: Another way to improve travel behavioural change. *Cities, 85*, 140–149.

Zainuddin, Z., Chu, S. K. W., Shujahat, M., & Perera, C. J. (2020). The impact of gamification on learning and instruction: A systematic review of empirical evidence. *Educational Research Review, 30*, 100326.

5 Ethical Issues in Gamification and Design Thinking in Higher Education

5.1 Introduction

In Chapter 2, we explored the main aspects of gamification, detailing the steps that must be followed to create a gamified experience in the context of higher education. Subsequently, we have dedicated Chapter 3 to design thinking. We examined how the design thinking process can be applied to activities in higher education and discussed two examples based on this resource. In Chapter 4, we analyzed the ways in which both techniques—gamification and design thinking—can be combined to create experiences in the context of higher education. In addition to explaining how these resources can be brought together, we explained in detail how the two examples of activities based on design thinking discussed in Chapter 3 can be gamified.

This chapter is devoted to ethical issues. Specifically, we analyze the main ethical issues that emerge in the field of higher education as well as issues related to the use of gamification and design thinking as educational tools.

5.2 Ethics and Higher Education

The study of ethics in higher education as well as of the responsibilities of all the agents involved in this field has been a relevant topic for decades (Brown & Krager, 1985; Couch & Dodd, 2005; Raman et al., 2023). García-Peñalvo (2021) highlights certain considerations that should be taken into account in the context of ethics in higher education, such as respect for licenses and the authorship of materials as well as the need to use tools to detect plagiarism and prevent this practice. These issues pertain to teachers and researchers as well as students. Teachers can use materials that are not their own without citing the source in addition to the possibility of committing plagiarism in their research. In addition, teachers can make different degrees of demands regarding the misconduct of their students.

Half of the university professors who participated in Palmer's study (2021) noted that they would accept work from their students in which 15% of the content was the result of plagiarism. In addition, most of these professors stated that they expected their students to plagiarize. Students may engage in plagiarism either intentionally or unintentionally. According to the study conducted by Farahian et al. (2022), differences in the frequency of plagiarism committed by university students from different countries are not the result of cultural differences but rather of other factors, such as the education these students have received in this regard. In many cases, students commit plagiarism because they do not know how to cite sources properly. Some students cite too many works to avoid being accused of plagiarism (Merkel, 2022).

Another problem is cheating on exams (Arab & Orfan, 2023). Amzalag et al. (2022) investigate academic integrity in the context of remotely administered exams. The most important result of the research conducted by these authors is that there is a lack of mutual trust between teachers and students. In addition, they highlight three reasons why students cheat on exams: because they do not want to fail and believe that they cannot pass the subject honestly; because they are dissatisfied with the teacher's work; and because the benefit they obtain from this practice is greater than the risk they face by engaging in it.

Digital tools are available to facilitate the detection of plagiarism and cheating in exams (Özşen et al., 2023). However, as Turnbull et al. (2021) note, these tools must be combined with the task of teaching students the ethical implications of engaging in this type of dishonest act. Amzalag et al. (2022) recommend engaging in dialog regarding the importance of ethical behavior with students, highlighting the value of this behavior and of the knowledge acquired thereby for their future performance in the working world, and encouraging teachers to set an example for their students and to serve as a model of ethical behavior.

García-Peñalvo (2021) emphasizes the importance of practices intended to curb plagiarism and respect authorship in the context of distance education. Via the internet, knowledge can more easily be disseminated. Perhaps this situation has made it easier for individuals to engage in plagiarism in the academic context. However, no empirical evidence indicates that plagiarism has increased in this context as a consequence of the popularization of the internet (Eaton, 2021).

Beyond their relationship with a possible increase in plagiarism, the fact is that the internet and other new technologies have transformed higher education. The term *e-learning* refers to the use of these resources in the context of teaching. However, since technology evolves rapidly and since higher education adopts emerging technology, no consensus has yet been reached regarding the definition of this term (Rodrigues et al., 2019). Moreover, the concepts of mobile learning (m-learning) and digital learning (d-learning) are often used as synonyms for e-learning (Kumar Basak et al., 2018). As Laufer et al. (2021) note, e-learning has facilitated access to the university environment for a large percentage of the population and for individuals at different stages of life. Other benefits of this technology are the possibility of adapting learning

Ethical Issues in Gamification and Design Thinking 79

paths and promoting collaboration among different agents in the context of higher education (Laufer et al., 2021).

The COVID-19 pandemic has forced individuals involved in higher education to shift their activity to the digital plane. The prevalence of e-learning increased from 14.5% per year globally prior to the pandemic to become present in 60% of educational institutions as a result of the COVID-19 pandemic (Alqahtani & Rajkhan, 2020). From the perspectives of students and university teachers, e-learning offers certain advantages but also poses a challenge. On the one hand, the student participants in the study conducted by Maatuk et al. (2022) argued that e-learning is useful and helps improve teaching. However, they also stated that it increases the pressure they face and that poor technological infrastructure acts as a barrier to the proper development of learning.

On the other hand, the university teachers who participated in the study conducted by Maatuk et al. (2022) noted that e-learning promotes the development of students' technological skills. Regarding the challenges associated with e-learning, the teachers highlighted its cost and the need for corresponding funding. Kulikowski et al. (2022) add that the forced transition to e-learning may have affected teachers negatively, as task identity, task significance, autonomy, and the social dimension of the work, among others, have decreased.

However, the main ethical problem associated with the use of digital technology in higher education is related to the digital divide (Devisakti et al., 2023). The concept of the digital divide emerged in the mid-1990s (Light, 2001). This term refers to "the gap between people who have adequate access to information communication technology (ICT) and people who have poor or no access to ICT" (Lythreatis et al., 2022). The digital divide can be separated into three levels (Gran et al., 2021). The first such level refers to the possibility of access, including the availability of devices based on digital technology—smartphones, computers, and so forth—and internet connections. The second level of the digital divide refers to the possession of the necessary technological skills by the individual. Finally, the third level refers to the question of whether these skills are beneficial.

That is, the digital divide pertains not only to the possession of digital devices and an internet connection but also to the digital skills or digital literacy of both teachers and students. Regarding students, the current generation of university students belongs to Generation Z. One characteristic of this population group is the intensive use of technology (Szymkowiak et al., 2021). In this context, we must bear in mind the differences that may exist among the particular environments that surround each student.

Mathrani et al. (2022) analyze the impact of the digital divide on education in developing countries during the COVID-19 pandemic. According to this research, in which 90% of the participants were pursuing university studies, more than half of the participants used cell phones to facilitate e-learning.

Regarding the type of connection they used, approximately half of the participants used mobile data. The percentage of students who used computers (personal or shared with other members of the household) and home broadband connections was much lower. In other words, the possibilities and resources differed among the participating students, with a large percentage facing certain limitations. Other studies, such as those conducted by Muflih et al. (2021) highlight the difficulties accessing the internet faced by a large percentage of university students.

Moreover, the digital divide has affected the mental health of people during the COVID-19 pandemic negatively, leading to stress, distress, and anxiety (Cheshmehzangi et al., 2022; Akingbade et al., 2023). Li and Yu (2022) analyze the ways in which the COVID-19 pandemic affected university professors by conducting a literature review. These authors find that the shift of education to the digital plane has increased the level of complexity associated with the work of teachers who taught face to face prior to the pandemic. In addition, their levels of satisfaction and well-being have decreased, leading to experiences of frustration and feelings of failure. These difficulties are related to the development of these teachers' digital skills. Li and Yu (2022) argue that the digital literacy of university teachers should be improved. The responsible agents—governments and other authorities—have created programs aimed at promoting the development of these teachers' digital skills. These programs should be used to improve both the quality of higher education and its digitization as well as to increase the satisfaction and well-being of teachers.

The review conducted by Basilotta-Gómez-Pablos et al. (2022) to investigate the digital skills of university teachers concludes that their level of these competencies is low or medium-low. This research also indicates that studies on this topic have increased significantly in recent years and that continuous learning and the creation of personalized digital skills teaching plans should be encouraged.

In summary, to take advantage of all the potential benefits of digital technology in the context of higher education, strategies must be developed to reduce the digital divide. Facilitating access to digital devices and internet connections as well as promoting the development of digital skills among both teachers and students are necessary tasks for the continuation of digitization. These tasks are closely related to gamification and design thinking. As discussed in previous chapters, these two resources can use digital technology to create more complete experiences.

For example, gamification can be introduced into courses through the use of gamified educational platforms such as Kahoot (McQuiston, 2023). We can create a quiz using the Kahoot platform that can be solved by learners in a gamified environment. In this context, it should be noted that students need a device with an internet connection as well as sufficient digital skills to be able to respond to such a quiz. Regarding design thinking, in the two examples presented in Chapters 3 and 4 of this book, we combine design thinking with the flipped classroom methodology. Specifically, students are required to perform a series of out-of-class activities between the sessions of each of the experiences. Some of these activities consist, for example, of watching videos. To be able to accomplish this task, students once again need a device with an internet connection and sufficient digital skills.

Therefore, when designing and developing our gamified design thinking activities, we must bear in mind the possible limitations resulting from the digital divide that may present a challenge for some students. Likewise, we must create strategies to ensure that the digital divide is not a detriment to these students and that they have the same possibilities to learn as the rest of their peers.

Another ethical issue in higher education pertains to privacy and the use of data. Numerous digital platforms that are currently used generate and host data regarding students. As a result of technological progress, we now have access to resources such as learning analytics. Learning analytics is based on the collection and analysis of data generated by students to predict their results and improve their individual learning abilities (Guzmán-Valenzuela et al., 2021). The problem in this context arises from the governance of these data and their potential use (Jones & Hinchliffe, 2023).

Holmes et al. (2022) highlight three issues pertaining to the ethics of educational data drawn from learning analytics. First, this issue has emerged recently, and the question of which behaviors are ethical has not yet been answered. Second, ethics in this context involves informed consent, data interpretation and management, user privacy, and surveillance, among other factors. Finally, some individuals stand against this practice due to concerns regarding its future consequences. Similarly, it is worth noting that the evidence regarding the ability of learning analytics to improve learning outcomes in higher education remains limited (Viberg et al., 2018). In any case, this issue affects both learning analytics platforms and other educational platforms in which student data are generated to a greater or lesser extent. Having outlined the most salient ethical issues in higher education, in the following sections, we discuss some ethical issues related to gamification and design thinking in this context.

5.3 Ethics and Gamification

As mentioned on several occasions throughout this book, most studies on gamification indicate that it generally has a positive influence on the motivation and engagement of individuals (Arufe-Giráldez et al., 2022; Xiao et al., 2022). However, other studies indicate negative results. These negative results are often referred to as the dark side of gamification (Almeida et al., 2023). While gamification provides many benefits, it also presents challenges to both students and teachers. Saleem et al. (2022) note that gamified activities require effort on the part of students and can be distracting and stressful

82 *Ethical Issues in Gamification and Design Thinking*

for them. These authors add that, as far as teachers are concerned, gamification also requires their effort. In addition, teachers may encounter problems related to infrastructure since, in some faculties, the technological equipment does not function properly.

Nyström (2021) conducts a literature review to investigate the negative side or "darkness" of gamification and organizes the problems thus identified on the basis of the following seven themes:

- Motivation. As mentioned throughout this book, gamification represents an attempt to influence the motivation of individuals to achieve a change in their behavior. However, the effect of gamification on the motivation of some users may be different from expected. We address this topic in further detail in this section.
- Addiction. The problem of game addiction has been widely studied (Han et al., 2022). A gamified design can also lead to addiction. Nyström (2021) recommends that designers should take precautions and establish mechanisms to avoid this problem, such as setting a maximum time of use or imposing breaks every 20 minutes.
- Competition and collaboration. Nyström (2021) notes that some designs that encourage competition among participants can be counterproductive and hinder collaboration among participants. This author recommends monitoring the level of competition to avoid affecting the achievement of gamification objectives negatively. As discussed in Chapter 2, the effects of gamification on learners are greater if competition and collaboration are combined than if only competition is used (Sailer & Homner, 2020). In addition, competition can generate pressure and reduce student motivation (Featherstone & Habgood, 2019).
- Manipulation. Gamification promotes certain behaviors in individuals. Sometimes, users of the gamified experience may feel as if they are being manipulated into performing an action in which they do not truly want to engage. In the field of education, gamification can take a paternalistic approach with the aim of promoting a behavior that is beneficial to students (Tep et al., 2021). However, we also find cases of potential unethical manipulative strategies that use gamification, for example, manipulative advertising (Martin, 2022).
- Data integrity. The protection of data obtained from users during their participation in a gamified experience is an ethical behavior on the part of those who are responsible for the experience. As mentioned in the previous section, the management of data generated on educational platforms is a recent issue, and no consensus has yet been reached regarding what is meant by ethical behavior in this context (Holmes et al., 2022; Jones & Hinchliffe, 2023).
- Surveillance and privacy. Some gamified designs can cause participants to feel as if they are being watched either by those responsible for the

gamified activity or by other participants, and this feeling can affect their well-being. Nyström (2021) recommends that designers should offer participants the possibility of choosing what information they want to share and thus help preserve their privacy.
- Ethics and exploitation. The persuasion of individuals can be viewed as a form of exploitation. This issue affects different areas, such as the gamification of work and even higher education. Nyström (2021) highlights the need for further research and the possibility of creating a regulatory framework in this context.

In recent years, research concerning the adverse or dark side effects of gamification has also increased in the field of education. According to the conducted review by Almeida et al. (2023), most studies in which a negative effect of gamification on students has been detected concern the domain of computer science, followed by the disciplines of medicine and business.

Metwally et al. (2021) conducted a literature review of gamification in education and concluded that its adverse effects include reduced student performance and motivation, low student engagement and sense of belonging, and the generation of anxiety and envy. The envy resulting from gamification may even cause some students to fail to help their friends due to the gamified design (Metwally et al., 2021), which occurs if competition takes precedence over collaboration. As Nyström (2021) notes, it is important to monitor the level of competition to prevent the gamification from impeding collaboration among students. In addition, competition can reduce students' motivation if it confronts them with a high level of pressure (Featherstone & Habgood, 2019).

Kwon and Özpolat (2021) developed an elaborate gamified design for the assessment activities associated with a course. Their experience includes rewards, teams, competition, and narrative based on the nomenclature assigned to the activities. They intended to use this design to improve students' content knowledge and their perceptions of the learning experience. However, contrary to expectations, the results of their study indicate that the content knowledge of the university students who participated in the gamified experience was lower than that of the control group. In addition, the students who participated in the gamified experience were less satisfied with the learning method used. In other words, gamification had a negative impact on the content knowledge and perceptions of university students in this context.

The negative effects of gamification have also been demonstrated in fields other than higher education. For example, in the context of the gamification of work, Hammedi et al. (2021) highlight the negative effects of gamification on employee engagement and well-being. In the domain of health care, Yang and Li (2021b) conclude that the competition and interactivity resulting from gamification are associated with an invasion of users' privacy as well as social overload.

Zahedi et al. (2021) conducted an empirical study to investigate the effects of gamification in higher education. One student participant in this study reported feeling demotivated due to the gamified design, particularly the scoring system on which it was based. Zahedi et al. (2021) argue that confusing designs can discourage participation, and these authors recommend establishing clear rules to mitigate a possible negative effect on student motivation.

Gamification can also influence variables other than learner motivation. Hadi Mogavi et al. (2022) investigate the negative consequences of gamification misuse on the user based on a gamified language learning application and user testimonials. These authors conclude that gamification can reduce learning. On the one hand, gamification can lead to a decrease in student confidence. One subject in the study reported that he lost confidence in his abilities when he realized that he did not answer any of the application's questions correctly, which was because he had previously cheated to get more points by answering previous questions correctly.

On the other hand, the misuse of gamification can reduce students' interest in learning. Hadi Mogavi et al. (2022) argue that some users experience stress if new challenges or goals to be achieved are added to the gamified application. This finding shows that these learners are more interested in achieving the gamified objectives than in their own learning. Another possible negative consequence of gamification misuse related to reduced learning pertains to the possibility of a student dropping out of school. A participant in the study conducted by Hadi Mogavi et al. (2022) stated that gamification was one of the causes underlying his dropping out of the language learning application.

Finally, it should be noted that some studies indicate that gamification has no effect on university students. Donnermann et al. (2021) investigate the influence of gamification and social robots on students' motivation and engagement. They conclude that neither gamification nor social robots have any effect on students' motivation and engagement. Moreover, these authors find that a combination of the two techniques has a negative influence on the engagement of university students.

The differences regarding the results of gamification across these different studies conducted in the educational environment are due to factors such as the gender of students as well as individual differences such as their personality or their experience of and resistance to the use of new technologies (Luo, 2022). In addition, research shows certain limitations or barriers in this context, such as the lack of a specific definition of gamification, a superficial or inadequate use of this technique, and methodological limitations (Luo, 2022).

On the other hand, in recent years, studies have begun to examine whether gamification can affect users' well-being negatively. For example, Hammedi et al. (2021) investigate whether the gamification of work can influence employee engagement and well-being negatively. Nyström (2021) defines dark gamification design as "the craft of purposefully designing gamification that do not have the well-being of the user in mind" (p. 3). In the field of education, Hadi Mogavi et al. (2022) highlight several possible negative effects of gamification on students' psychological and physical well-being. Regarding psychological well-being, gamification can lead to disappointment, apprehension, and self-recrimination. Disappointment occurs when user expectations are not met. Apprehension refers to the stress or anxiety that can be generated by the system. Finally, self-recrimination is related to situations in which the participant feels guilty after overusing the gamified system and becoming aware of his or her obsession.

Regarding the possible negative effects of gamification on the physical well-being of students, Hadi Mogavi et al. (2022) highlight two issues: problems with physical health and changes in daily routines. In the context of physical health, gamification, like video games, can lead to problems, for example, problems resulting from poor body posture during intensive use of the gamified system. Finally, gamification can elicit addiction and, as a result, lead to a change in routines. This process can have a negative impact on the physical well-being of users.

The possible negative effects of gamified experiences on the physical well-being of participants have rarely been analyzed by academics. The negative effects of gamified experiences on psychological well-being, on the other hand, have attracted attention from researchers. Chen et al. (2022) study the possible negative effect of gamification on the learning emotions of university students and conclude that it does not exert a significant effect on students' anxiety or cognitive load. López-Martínez et al. (2022) find that the use of gamification in higher education increases students' interest and decreases perceived stress and pressure.

Finally, some authors argue that gamification can be viewed as a type of manipulation. Tep et al. (2021, p. 214) claim that gamification "can be considered as a type of nudge, that is, an architecture of choices for guiding individuals in their decision-making processes." The ethical debate in this context revolves around paternalistic nudges. These nudges do not focus on educating individuals, nor do they grant those individuals autonomy. In contrast, such nudges guide decision-making by depriving individuals of their freedom to choose between different options. This paternalism, while it is aimed at improving the welfare of the individual, remains controversial (Tep et al., 2021).

Through gamification, users can be manipulated, and their behavior can be modified. Gorin (2022) notes that gamification manipulates individuals and limits their decision-making capacity and behavior. However, this manipulation via gamification can occur even in situations in which the individuals who are responsible for the experience do not do so deliberately or intentionally (Kriz et al., 2022). In any case, as Kim and Werbach (2022) note, managers must monitor and take action to correct designs that manipulate users, even if such manipulation occurs unintentionally. Otherwise, the managers' actions would be unethical. In the following, we address the ethical issues related to design thinking.

5.4 Ethics and Design Thinking

The specialized literature contains few references to ethics in the context of the application of design thinking in higher education. This lack may be due to the fact that the use of design thinking in this context remains limited, and the study of the ethics surrounding this topic remains underdeveloped. Therefore, in this section, we analyze different questions pertaining to ethics and design thinking in general, mainly in the organizational field, as well as the relationship between ethics and the application of design thinking in higher education.

Carlgren and BenMahmoud-Jouini (2022, p. 44) analyze the conflicts that can arise between the values and assumptions associated with design thinking and the culture of the organization into which such thinking is introduced. These authors identify eight cultural characteristics and highlight the challenges associated with each of them. These eight cultural characteristics are "subjective and aesthetic ways of knowing; long-term and nonlinear views of time; intrinsic motivation and sense of purpose; flexibility and change; relationships, empathy, and emotions at work; collaboration and inclusion; team autonomy and informality; and external orientation."

First, regarding subjective and aesthetic ways of knowing, according to the design thinking approach, truth is subjective, and knowledge is obtained via the senses. This approach can generate a lack of legitimacy in traditional organizations in which quantitative results are predominant, which may conflict with the subjective and aesthetic vision of design thinking. Second, the long-term and nonlinear views regarding time associated with design thinking may clash with the need of organizations to obtain fast and effective results. In such a case, the lack of depth poses a challenge. Third, design thinking focuses on intrinsic motivation and the creation of a sense of purpose. A challenge emerges when employees do not feel as if they are engaged and when the economic incentives offered to them by the organization fail to motivate them (Carlgren & BenMahmoud-Jouini, 2022).

Fourth, design thinking is aimed at ensuring flexibility and adaptation in an environment of uncertainty. This goal can lead to conflict in organizations that resist change. Fifth, design thinking requires relationships and empathy among employees. In organizations in which the social dimension of work is not promoted, design thinking can be viewed as an unserious activity. Sixth, design thinking focuses on collaboration. This focus can lead to conflict in organizations in which individual work is the norm. Seventh, design thinking requires organizations to trust employees and give them autonomy. Conflict arises in organizations in which power is centralized and in which excessive control is exercised over workers. Eighth and finally, design thinking maintains that to facilitate innovation, one must have an external orientation. In this case, a challenge arises with respect to organizations that exhibit an internal orientation that does not value the opinions and knowledge of external agents (Carlgren & BenMahmoud-Jouini, 2022).

When designing a design thinking experience in higher education, we must bear in mind the characteristics and conflicts identified by Carlgren and BenMahmoud-Jouini (2022). For example, the third characteristic pertains to design thinking's focus on intrinsic motivation and the creation of a sense of purpose. These authors argue that this task can be challenging if employees are not motivated and engaged. If we apply this argument to higher education, we can see that a challenge emerges if students do not feel motivated to participate in a design thinking activity. To solve this problem, we must design mechanisms that influence students' motivation, such as the other technique that is the subject of this book: gamification.

Returning to the topic of ethics, Hamington (2019) relates design thinking to care ethics. This author defines the term *care* as "performed acts that promote the well-being and flourishing of others and ourselves based on knowledge and responsiveness to the one cared for" (Hamington, 2019, p. 92). Hamington (2019) argues that care ethics can incorporate an explicit moral narrative into design thinking. Design thinking focuses on innovation, empathy, and problem-solving. Relying on a moral narrative would lead to what this author calls "caring design." Specifically, Hamington (2019) defines caring design as "a human-centered innovation and problem solving methodology/process as well as a moral and epistemological ideal grounded in a commitment to inquiry, empathy, and care for constituent stakeholders" (p. 97). Unlike human-centered design, caring design is based on commitment and trust.

As previously noted, the literature contains few references to ethics and design thinking in the context of higher education. Lake et al. (2021) examine the opinions of 35 faculty members concerning a design thinking initiative in higher education. Their study shows that the negative outcomes of design thinking as perceived by the participants include student frustration with ambiguity, resistance to nonlinear processes, lack of trust in the process, time constraints, and anxiety regarding outcomes. Although additional studies are necessary to corroborate the results found by Lake et al. (2021), these results serve as a warning of certain negative results of the implementation of our design thinking activity in higher education. Therefore, it is advisable to bear these warnings in mind and to design mechanisms to avoid the corresponding dangers.

In other words, to avoid frustrating students due to the ambiguity of the activity, we must clearly establish the terms of the activity as well as its objective. In the two examples discussed in Chapters 3 and 4 of this book, we dedicate an initial session to the task of explaining the project to the students as well as its aims, the ways in which it will be carried out, and the manner in which it will be assessed. Another negative effect is detected by Lake et al. (2021). In our examples, we combine design thinking, gamification, and the flipped classroom methodology. Using the flipped classroom methodology, traditional lectures can be converted into work that the student accomplishes before class and outside the classroom, thus allowing the time spent inside the classroom to be devoted to practical activities (Galindo-Domínguez, 2021; Hew et al., 2021). As a result, more time is available to facilitate the sessions corresponding to the different phases of design thinking within the classroom, and the students are prepared to participate in these sessions as a result of their previous work. In any case, we must ensure that the time allocated to each session is sufficient and, if not, modify the design of our activity.

McLaughlin et al. (2022) analyze the application of design thinking to different disciplines in four universities. These authors highlight four outcomes of design thinking: implementation support, psychological benefits and motivation, relationships and trust, the quality of the solutions generated, and individual adaptation and flexibility. On the theme of ethics, McLaughlin et al. (2022) note that most students experience psychological benefits and motivation in this context. Additionally, the results suggest that these benefits are more common if design thinking is taught explicitly. This category of outcomes encompasses increased confidence in creative skills and the commitment of group members as well as their motivation to continue engaging in the activity, among other factors.

Psychological benefits are closely related to students' well-being (Yurayat & Seechaliao, 2021). According to Seijts et al. (2022), the subjective well-being of university students also depends on their character. Furthermore, each student is surrounded by particular circumstances, which also influence their behavior and the ways in which they cope with the events they experience (Mulvogue et al., 2022). Moreover, university professors also influence students' well-being due to the importance of their benevolence, the support they provide, their availability, and their competence, among other factors (Eloff et al., 2021).

Wolcott et al. (2021) provide 12 tips for the creation of design thinking-based activities in the education of future physicians. These tips are as follows:

1. Collect materials to develop your design thinking knowledge and capabilities.
2. Engage with the design thinking philosophy.
3. Begin with a warm-up activity.
4. Connect with people and be perceptive.
5. Ask yourself if you have delimited the problem properly and modify it if necessary.
6. Draw inspiration from other subjects, especially those that appear to be unrelated to the topic at hand.
7. Prototype potential solutions and request feedback regarding possible enhancements.
8. Change your standard approach to thinking and separate the processes.
9. Employ different methods of storytelling and displaying ideas.

Ethical Issues in Gamification and Design Thinking 89

10. Foster collaboration and teamwork by promoting trust and psychological safety and normalize failure.
11. Incorporate playfulness and leisure into the process.
12. Instruct others in design thinking.

All these tips are useful for teachers and agents who are responsible for higher education and who are interested in developing educational activities based on design thinking. In this chapter, we focus on the ethical aspects of this process. Therefore, tip number ten is of special interest. Design thinking focuses on teamwork. Wolcott et al. (2021) recommend the creation of a pleasant climate in which participants feel comfortable with other team members and do not feel judged. Accordingly, trust and psychological safety should be promoted.

In Chapter 4, we demonstrated how to gamify two examples of activities based on design thinking. We commented that to enable students to take advantage of their talents and develop original ideas, a climate of trust must be created in which they are not judged. Therefore, it is not advisable to introduce competitive social interactions in this context. Instead, we should promote collaborative work to facilitate cocreation. Furthermore, Wolcott et al. (2021) emphasize the importance of normalizing failure and providing students with the necessary tools to accept failure and continue to improve, thereby fostering a growth mindset.

According to the study conducted by Nunes et al. (2022), college students' fear of failure stems mainly from the expectations of their family members (37%), their own expectations and standards (23%), and the expectations of third parties who seem to judge them (18%). Nunes et al. (2022) also identify the measures that students believe should be taken to reduce their fear of failure. These measures include communication regarding failure and resilience (47%) and the redesign of subjects to allow students to correct their failures (41%).

Regarding the expectations and fear of failure of college students, Law and Finnigan (2021) recommend modifying expectations, including both the expectations of the students themselves and those of others, as well as making those expectations flexible. Having flexible expectations includes an awareness of the possibility of failure before beginning a task, which is intended to reduce the stigma associated with a potential failure. In addition, a plan for dealing with failure can be created to guide learners in such a scenario.

As Sahagun et al. (2021) note, failure is an inevitable component of our lives, and success is determined by our response to failure. Individuals with a fixed mindset experience thoughts of task abandonment when they fail and do not consider the possibility of striving to improve. On the other hand, individuals with a growth mindset view this situation as an opportunity to learn and develop their capabilities. Sahagun et al. (2021) propose five actions that teachers can use to encourage university students to develop a growth mindset: (i) identify the classroom as a place in which students train, (ii) ask students to complete homework prior to class, (iii) provide students with feedback on a weekly basis to indicate how they are performing and ways in which they can improve their performance, (iv) allow students the freedom to make mistakes, and (v) offer students opportunities to improve. All of these recommendations and tips can be incorporated into our design thinking activity to promote students' learning by allowing them to correct their mistakes in a judgment-free environment in which they feel comfortable.

Finally, design thinking can be applied to the teaching of ethics in higher education. Marcus et al. (2020) create an activity based on design thinking and develop it in the context of medical ethics education. Specifically, Marcus et al. (2020) design an activity intended to teach students the ethical implications of organ transplantation. The experience lasts 90 minutes, encompasses all phases of the design thinking process, and is implemented collaboratively with the participation of teams of students. Marcus et al. (2020) conclude that this activity can improve students' knowledge of organ transplantation and the design thinking process. Regarding possibilities for improvement, some students highlighted the need to improve the way in which the activity was guided as well as to modify its duration to increase the time devoted to some of the phases. This finding is consistent with the results of the study conducted by Akgul et al. (2021), who analyzed the opinions of participants in a design thinking activity in the context of higher education. Akgul et al. (2021) note that although design thinking offers different benefits, some of the participants in their activity reported frustration due to the duration of the experience as well as its difficulty.

In summary, several aspects of ethics are relevant to higher education, gamification, and design thinking. In this chapter, we discussed the most relevant issues in this context. Subsequently, we discuss our conclusion and final thoughts in the final chapter of this book.

References

Akingbade, O., Adeleye, K., Fadodun, O. A., Fawole, I. O., Li, J., Choi, E. P. H., . . . Ogungbe, O. (2023). eHealth literacy was associated with anxiety and depression during the COVID-19 pandemic in Nigeria: A cross-sectional study. *Frontiers in Public Health, 11*, 1194908.

Akgul, T., Brown, J., Milz, B., & Messina, K. (2021). Design thinking applied in higher education: Exploring participant experiences. *Journal of Design Thinking, 2*(1), 37–44.

Almeida, C., Kalinowski, M., Uchôa, A., & Feijó, B. (2023). Negative effects of gamification in education software: Systematic mapping and practitioner perceptions. *Information and Software Technology, 156*, 107142.

Alqahtani, A. Y., & Rajkhan, A. A. (2020). E-learning critical success factors during the covid-19 pandemic: A comprehensive analysis of e-learning managerial perspectives. *Education Sciences, 10*(9), 216.

Amzalag, M., Shapira, N., & Dolev, N. (2022). Two sides of the coin: Lack of academic integrity in exams during the corona pandemic, students' and lecturers' perceptions. *Journal of Academic Ethics, 20*(2), 243–263.

Arab, S., & Orfan, S. N. (2023). Perceptions of Afghan EFL undergraduate students about exam cheating. *Cogent Arts & Humanities, 10*(1), 2215564.

Arufe-Giráldez, V., Sanmiguel-Rodríguez, A., Ramos-Álvarez, O., & Navarro-Patón, R. (2022). Gamification in physical education: A systematic review. *Education Sciences, 12*(8), 540.

Basilotta-Gómez-Pablos, V., Matarranz, M., Casado-Aranda, L. A., & Otto, A. (2022). Teachers' digital competencies in higher education: A systematic literature review. *International Journal of Educational Technology in Higher Education, 19*, 8.

Brown, R. D., & Krager, L. (1985). Ethical issues in graduate education: Faculty and student responsibilities. *The Journal of Higher Education, 56*(4), 403–418.

Carlgren, L., & BenMahmoud-Jouini, S. (2022). When cultures collide: What can we learn from frictions in the implementation of design thinking? *Journal of Product Innovation Management, 39*(1), 44–65.

Chen, Y., Zhang, L., & Yin, H. (2022). A longitudinal study on students' foreign language anxiety and cognitive load in gamified classes of higher education. *Sustainability, 14*(17), 10905.

Cheshmehzangi, A., Zou, T., & Su, Z. (2022). The digital divide impacts on mental health during the COVID-19 pandemic. *Brain, Behavior, and Immunity, 101*, 211–213.

Couch, S., & Dodd, S. (2005). Doing the right thing: Ethical issues in higher education. *Journal of Family and Consumer Sciences, 97*(3), 20.

Devisakti, A., Muftahu, M., & Xiaoling, H. (2023). Digital divide among B40 students in Malaysian higher education institutions. *Education and Information Technologies*. doi:10.1007/s10639-023-11847-w

Donnermann, M., Lein, M., Messingschlager, T., Riedmann, A., Schaper, P., Steinhaeusser, S., & Lugrin, B. (2021). Social robots and gamification for technology supported learning: An empirical study on engagement and motivation. *Computers in Human Behavior, 121*, 106792.

Eaton, S. E. (2021). *Plagiarism in higher education: Tackling tough topics in academic integrity*. Santa Barbara, California, US: ABC-CLIO.

Eloff, I., O'Neil, S., & Kanengoni, H. (2021). Students' well-being in tertiary environments: Insights into the (unrecognised) role of lecturers. *Teaching in Higher Education, 28*(7), 1777–1793.

Farahian, M., Avarzamani, F., & Rezaee, M. (2022). Plagiarism in higher education across nations: A case of language students. *Journal of Applied Research in Higher Education, 14*(1), 223–239.

Featherstone, M., & Habgood, J. (2019). UniCraft: Exploring the impact of asynchronous multiplayer game elements in gamification. *International Journal of Human-Computer Studies, 127*, 150–168.

Galindo-Domínguez, H. (2021). Flipped classroom in the educational system. *Educational Technology & Society, 24*(3), 44–60.

García-Peñalvo, F. J. (2021). Avoiding the dark side of digital transformation in teaching. An institutional reference framework for eLearning in higher education. *Sustainability, 13*(4), 2023.

Gorin, M. (2022). Gamification, manipulation, and domination 1. In *The philosophy of online manipulation* (pp. 199–215). New York, NY, US: Routledge.

Gran, A. B., Booth, P., & Bucher, T. (2021). To be or not to be algorithm aware: A question of a new digital divide? *Information, Communication & Society*, *24*(12), 1779–1796.

Guzmán-Valenzuela, C., Gómez-González, C., Rojas-Murphy Tagle, A., & Lorca-Vyhmeister, A. (2021). Learning analytics in higher education: A preponderance of analytics but very little learning? *International Journal of Educational Technology in Higher Education*, *18*, 23.

Hadi Mogavi, R., Guo, B., Zhang, Y., Haq, E. U., Hui, P., & Ma, X. (2022, June). When gamification spoils your learning: A qualitative case study of gamification misuse in a language-learning app. In *Proceedings of the ninth ACM conference on learning@ scale* (pp. 175–188). New York, US: Association for Computing Machinery.

Hamington, M. (2019). Integrating care ethics and design thinking. *Journal of Business Ethics*, *155*, 91–103.

Hammedi, W., Leclercq, T., Poncin, I., & Alkire, L. (2021). Uncovering the dark side of gamification at work: Impacts on engagement and well-being. *Journal of Business Research*, *122*, 256–269.

Han, T. S., Cho, H., Sung, D., & Park, M. H. (2022). A systematic review of the impact of COVID-19 on the game addiction of children and adolescents. *Frontiers in Psychiatry*, *13*, 976601.

Hew, K. F., Bai, S., Dawson, P., & Lo, C. K. (2021). Meta-analyses of flipped classroom studies: A review of methodology. *Educational Research Review*, *33*, 100393.

Holmes, W., Porayska-Pomsta, K., Holstein, K., Sutherland, E., Baker, T., Shum, S. B., ... Koedinger, K. R. (2022). Ethics of AI in education: Towards a community-wide framework. *International Journal of Artificial Intelligence in Education*, *32*(3), 504–526.

Jones, K. M., & Hinchliffe, L. J. (2023). Ethical issues and learning analytics: Are academic library practitioners prepared? *The Journal of Academic Librarianship*, *49*(1), 102621.

Kim, T. W., & Werbach, K. (2022). Excerpt from ethics of gamification. In *Ethics of data and analytics* (pp. 375–385). Boca Raton, Florida, US: Auerbach Publications.

Kriz, W. C., Kikkawa, T., & Sugiura, J. (2022). Manipulation through gamification and gaming. In *Gaming as a cultural commons* (pp. 185–199). Singapore: Springer.

Kulikowski, K., Przytuła, S., & Sułkowski, Ł. (2022). E-learning? Never again! On the unintended consequences of COVID-19 forced e-learning on academic teacher motivational job characteristics. *Higher Education Quarterly*, *76*(1), 174–189.

Kumar Basak, S., Wotto, M., & Belanger, P. (2018). E-learning, M-learning and D-learning: Conceptual definition and comparative analysis. *E-learning and Digital Media*, *15*(4), 191–216.

Kwon, H. Y., & Özpolat, K. (2021). The dark side of narrow gamification: Negative impact of assessment gamification on student perceptions and content knowledge. *INFORMS Transactions on Education*, *21*(2), 67–81.

Lake, D., Flannery, K., & Kearns, M. (2021). A cross-disciplines and cross-sector mixed-methods examination of design thinking practices and outcome. *Innovative Higher Education*, *46*(3), 337–356.

Laufer, M., Leiser, A., Deacon, B., Perrin de Brichambaut, P., Fecher, B., Kobsda, C., & Hesse, F. (2021). Digital higher education: A divider or bridge builder? Leadership perspectives on edtech in a COVID-19 reality. *International Journal of Educational Technology in Higher Education*, *18*, 51.

Law, M. P., & Finnigan, J. K. (2021). Letting your students fail: Overcoming failure experiences in undergraduate work-integrated learning. *International Journal of Work-Integrated Learning, 22*(3), 357–368.

Li, M., & Yu, Z. (2022). Teachers' satisfaction, role, and digital literacy during the COVID-19 pandemic. *Sustainability, 14*(3), 1121.

Light, J. (2001). Rethinking the digital divide. *Harvard Educational Review, 71*(4), 709–734.

López-Martínez, A., Meroño, L., Cánovas-López, M., García-de-Alcaraz, A., & Martínez-Aranda, L. M. (2022). Using gamified strategies in higher education: Relationship between intrinsic motivation and contextual variables. *Sustainability, 14*(17), 11014.

Luo, Z. (2022). Gamification for educational purposes: What are the factors contributing to varied effectiveness? *Education and Information Technologies, 27*, 891–915.

Lythreatis, S., Singh, S. K., & El-Kassar, A. N. (2022). The digital divide: A review and future research agenda. *Technological Forecasting and Social Change, 175*, 121359.

Maatuk, A. M., Elberkawi, E. K., Aljawarneh, S., Rashaideh, H., & Alharbi, H. (2022). The COVID-19 pandemic and E-learning: Challenges and opportunities from the perspective of students and instructors. *Journal of Computing in Higher Education, 34*, 21–38.

Marcus, D., Simone, A., & Block, L. (2020). Design thinking in medical ethics education. *Journal of Medical Ethics, 46*(4), 282–284.

Martin, K. (2022). Gamification, manipulation, and data analytics. In *Ethics of data and analytics* (pp. 357–361). Farnham, UK: Auerbach Publications.

Mathrani, A., Sarvesh, T., & Umer, R. (2022). Digital divide framework: Online learning in developing countries during the COVID-19 lockdown. *Globalisation, Societies and Education, 20*(5), 625–640.

McLaughlin, J. E., Chen, E., Lake, D., Guo, W., Skywark, E. R., Chernik, A., & Liu, T. (2022). Design thinking teaching and learning in higher education: Experiences across four universities. *PLoS One, 17*(3), e0265902.

McQuiston, J. M. (2023). Implimenting Kahoot! Into undergraduate political science courses. *Political Science Today, 3*(2), 20–21.

Merkel, W. (2022). Simple, yet complex: Pre-service teachers' conceptions of plagiarism at a Norwegian university. *Scandinavian Journal of Educational Research, 66*(6), 923–935.

Metwally, A. H. S., Nacke, L. E., Chang, M., Wang, Y., & Yousef, A. M. F. (2021). Revealing the hotspots of educational gamification: An umbrella review. *International Journal of Educational Research, 109*, 101832.

Muflih, S., Abuhammad, S., Al-Azzam, S., Alzoubi, K. H., Muflih, M., & Karasneh, R. (2021). Online learning for undergraduate health professional education during COVID-19: Jordanian medical students' attitudes and perceptions. *Heliyon, 7*(9), e08031.

Mulvogue, J., Ryan, C., Hunt, S., Cross, M., & Cleary, M. (2022). Promoting positive outcomes in higher education: Supporting undergraduate student mental health and well-being. *Issues in Mental Health Nursing, 44*(7), 673–677.

Nunes, K., Du, S., Philip, R., Mourad, M. M., Mansoor, Z., Laliberté, N., & Rawle, F. (2022). Science students' perspectives on how to decrease the stigma of failure. *FEBS Open Bio, 12*(1), 24–37.

Nyström, T. (2021). Exploring the darkness of gamification: You want it darker? In *Intelligent computing* (pp. 491–506). Cham: Springer.

Özşen, T., Saka, İ., Çelik, Ö., Razı, S., Akkan, S. Ç., & Dlabolova, D. H. (2023). Testing of support tools to detect plagiarism in academic Japanese texts. *Education and Information Technologies, 28*, 13287–13321.

Palmer, A. (2021). Investigating staff views on plagiarism in transnational higher education. *Journal of Applied Learning and Teaching, 4*(2), 13–27.

Raman, R., Utts, J., Cohen, A. I., & Hayat, M. J. (2023). Integrating ethics into the guidelines for assessment and instruction in statistics education (GAISE). *The American Statistician, 77*(3), 323–330.

Rodrigues, H., Almeida, F., Figueiredo, V., & Lopes, S. L. (2019). Tracking e-learning through published papers: A systematic review. *Computers & Education, 136*, 87–98.

Sahagun, M. A., Moser, R., Shomaker, J., & Fortier, J. (2021). Developing a growth-mindset pedagogy for higher education and testing its efficacy. *Social Sciences & Humanities Open, 4*(1), 100168.

Sailer, M., & Homner, L. (2020). The gamification of learning: A meta-analysis. *Educational Psychology Review, 32*, 77–112.

Saleem, A. N., Noori, N. M., & Ozdamli, F. (2022). Gamification applications in e-learning: A literature review. *Technology, Knowledge and Learning, 27*, 139–159.

Seijts, G. H., Monzani, L., Woodley, H. J., & Mohan, G. (2022). The effects of character on the perceived stressfulness of life events and subjective well-being of undergraduate business students. *Journal of Management Education, 46*(1), 106–139.

Szymkowiak, A., Melović, B., Dabić, M., Jeganathan, K., & Kundi, G. S. (2021). Information technology and Gen Z: The role of teachers, the internet, and technology in the education of young people. *Technology in Society, 65*, 101565.

Tep, S. P., Cachecho, M., & Jean-Bouchard, É. (2021). Innovation, ethics, and consumer protection: The context of fintech gamification in Quebec. In *Ubiquitous technologies for human development and knowledge management* (pp. 208–224). Hershey, Pennsylvania, US: IGI Global.

Turnbull, D., Chugh, R., & Luck, J. (2021). Transitioning to e-learning during the COVID-19 pandemic: How have Higher Education Institutions responded to the challenge? *Education and Information Technologies, 26*(5), 6401–6419.

Viberg, O., Hatakka, M., Bälter, O., & Mavroudi, A. (2018). The current landscape of learning analytics in higher education. *Computers in Human Behavior, 89*, 98–110.

Wolcott, M. D., McLaughlin, J. E., Hubbard, D. K., Rider, T. R., & Umstead, K. (2021). Twelve tips to stimulate creative problem-solving with design thinking. *Medical Teacher, 43*(5), 501–508.

Xiao, R., Wu, Z., & Hamari, J. (2022). Internet-of-gamification: A review of literature on IoT-enabled gamification for user engagement. *International Journal of Human–Computer Interaction, 38*(12), 1113–1137.

Yang, H., & Li, D. (2021b). Understanding the dark side of gamification health management: A stress perspective. *Information Processing & Management, 58*(5), 102649.

Yurayat, P., & Seechaliao, T. (2021). Effectiveness of online positive psychology intervention on psychological well-being among undergraduate students. *Journal of Education and Learning, 10*(4), 143–155.

Zahedi, L., Batten, J., Ross, M., Potvin, G., Damas, S., Clarke, P., & Davis, D. (2021). Gamification in education: A mixed-methods study of gender on computer science students' academic performance and identity development. *Journal of Computing in Higher Education, 33*(2), 441–474.

6 Conclusion and Final Reflections

This book aims to analyze the use of gamification and design thinking in higher education. With this purpose in mind, this last chapter presents this research work's main conclusion and final reflections.

First, it can be stated that gamification is a technique of particular relevance in the educational field since it enables both the motivation and engagement of students (Klock et al., 2020; Bouchrika et al., 2021; Murillo-Zamorano et al., 2021). It also enables behavioral changes that can be seen materialized in a boost in learning outcomes and academic performance (Sailer & Homner, 2020; Kim & Castelli, 2021; Zahedi et al., 2021). In this way, gamification creates motivating experiences with game-like elements in which there is an interaction among participants and where long-term objectives are established, seeking to complement the pedagogical system used and influence user engagement (Duggal et al., 2021; Fontana, 2020: Krath et al., 2021).

Chapter 2 explains in detail how to gamify a higher education activity (Cechetti et al., 2019; De la Peña et al., 2021; Deterding, 2015). In the analysis stage, we have shown the importance of examining the activity to be gamified and its context, how the objectives to be achieved with this activity condition the possibilities of the design, and above all, the analysis of the future participants. In the design and development stage, the gamification applied in previous similar activities has been studied a priori, and attention has also been paid to the result achieved in those circumstances. In this way, it is possible to conceive how the gamified experience will be and how it will be developed. In this sense, it has been explained how to establish the elements that are part of the gamified experience, how to maintain the participants' interest over time, and the possible use of platforms that enable these experiences to connect more easily with the students.

In the last stage, implementation and evaluation, attention was initially focused on the usefulness of carrying out a pilot study of the gamified experience so that possible problems can be detected and modifications can be made to improve the experience. The need for considering the gamified design as flexible and that it can be modified in the course of its use with the students to try to improve it has also been highlighted. In other words,

DOI: 10.4324/9781032675558-6

the key is to understand that it is not necessary to wait until the end of the gamified experience to evaluate its effects but that it can be checked as it is being carried out. All this does not preclude recognizing the need for a more exhaustive evaluation of the results achieved when the gamified experience has concluded. Determining whether or not there have been errors and considering possible improvements to be introduced in the gamified design is of vital importance to continuously improve the process to be carried out for gamification.

Second, it is worth remembering that this book deals with gamification and design thinking in higher education. Therefore, after examining the main conclusion of Chapter 2 referring to gamification, we will now focus on those of Chapter 3, which is dedicated to design thinking. In this sense, it has been explained that design thinking helps solve problems through innovation, even offering a step-by-step process that helps generate valuable solutions for stakeholders (Matthews & Wrigley, 2017; Laundry, 2020; Han, 2022). After succinctly going through the recent history of the term and examining the main models, the focus has been put on how design thinking can be helpful in higher education.

It has been explained that design thinking can boost in students a series of skills demanded in the labor market of the 21st century, such as collaboration and teamwork, creativity, problem-solving, and empathy (Scheer et al., 2012; Guaman-Quintanilla et al., 2018; Luka, 2019). It has also been specified how to raise a design thinking process in the field of higher education, but not without first highlighting, on the one hand, that diversity will have to be taken into account, given that no specific design thinking tool serves for everyone and is applicable in all circumstances; and on the other hand, that the design thinking proposal must be sustainable, seeking at all times that the participants are satisfied with the experience and the results that derive from it. Other additional aspects to consider before starting the design thinking activity plan are that the work must be planned around a real work project, that projects will not have a unique solution, and that collaborative work will be necessary.

Regarding the design thinking process roadmap, a proposal for action has been explained in Chapter 3, with a series of key questions to be considered in each stage of the design thinking process to be carried out by the educator. These key questions are referred to What?, Why? and How? Once these questions have been answered, the next step is to have access to a toolbox that makes it possible to implement the design thinking process and reach its various objectives. For the readers interested in going deeper into this area, in Chapter 3, we also provide them with recent literature in such area and also with a list of online platforms of great added value where they can go for more detailed knowledge of the main tools and resources that can be used to apply design thinking processes.

Conclusions and Final Reflections 97

Furthermore, in Chapter 3, two detailed examples are provided to explain how to apply design thinking in higher education: the first involves using design thinking to explore how international institutions influence the economy, society, and relationships in the world; the second focuses on how design thinking is used to involve students, faculty, and staff in improving a school, college, or organization. In the explanation of both examples, the Stanford d.school model is followed, and a flipped learning structure is used.

Both examples illustrate, in the first case, that through a design thinking process, students develop their design and non-design skills to propose a creative solution to a real-world problem; and in the second case, that students build community and have the opportunity to express their opinions about a shared situation. This way, giving students a voice has been achieved through a structured process to increase their empowerment. Chapter 3 concludes with a series of insights about how design thinking can help universities to evolve. Here is where it is advanced that the introduction of gamification elements in the design thinking process can be beneficial.

Third, having examined gamification and design thinking in depth in Chapters 2 and 3, respectively, Chapter 4 discusses how both techniques can be used simultaneously in higher education. In this sense, the literature review has identified the potential of combining them, given that they grant freedom to designers to adapt them to the idiosyncratic characteristics where they are to be applied and take into account individuals, promoting their motivation, engagement, and participation (Hung, 2018; Villegas et al., 2019; Kessing & Löwer, 2021; Patrício et al., 2021).

It has also been explained that to gamify an activity based on a design thinking process, the same stages must be considered in Section 2.3, while at the same time, the five phases of the popular design thinking model of Stanford d.school, examined in Section 3.3.3, must be considered. Implementing this fusion of techniques (gamification and design thinking) in higher education has been materialized with two extensively detailed examples. In particular, a redesign of the two described examples of design thinking from Chapter 3 is made, incorporating in Chapter 4 elements of gamification according to the five phases of the design thinking model of Stanford d.school. This provides valuable recommendations and insights for academia in the analysis, design and development, and implementation and evaluation of gamified design thinking activities to be carried out in higher education.

Finally, Chapter 5 examined the ethical aspects linked to gamification and design thinking. In general, it can be stated that one of the main ethical issues arising from the use of digital technology in higher education is the digital divide, thus making it necessary to provide students with access to digital devices and Internet connection while promoting the development of their digital skills (Gran et al., 2021; Mathrani et al., 2022; Muflih et al., 2021). Another relevant ethical aspect considered has been privacy and data use, where it has become clear that this is a recent issue and where further work is needed to understand better the terms about what behaviors are ethical within this field (Guzmán-Valenzuela et al., 2021).

Likewise, concerning the two examples in Chapter 4 on how to gamify activities based on design thinking, from an ethical perspective, Chapter 5 indicates the need to create a climate of trust and psychological safety in which participants feel comfortable so that students release their talent and contribute with original ideas (Law & Finnigan, 2021; Wolcott et al., 2021). Thus, competitive social interactions should not be overemphasized if the aim is to promote collaborative work and foster growth-minded co-creation (Sahagun et al., 2021; Wolcott et al., 2021).

References

Bouchrika, I., Harrati, N., Wanick, V., & Wills, G. (2021). Exploring the impact of gamification on student engagement and involvement with e-learning systems. *Interactive Learning Environments*, *29*(8), 1244–1257.

Cechetti, N. P., Bellei, E. A., Biduski, D., Rodriguez, J. P. M., Roman, M. K., & De Marchi, A. C. B. (2019). Developing and implementing a gamification method to improve user engagement: A case study with an m-Health application for hypertension monitoring. *Telematics and Informatics*, *41*, 126–138.

de la Peña, D., Lizcano, D., & Martínez-Álvarez, I. (2021). Learning through play: Gamification model in university-level distance learning. *Entertainment Computing*, *39*, 100430.

Deterding, S. (2015). The lens of intrinsic skill atoms: A method for gameful design. *Human–Computer Interaction*, *30*(3–4), 294–335.

Duggal, K., Singh, P., & Gupta, L. R. (2021). Impact of gamification, games, and game elements in education. In *Innovations in information and communication technologies (IICT-2020)* (pp. 201–210). Cham: Springer.

Fontana, M. T. (2020). Gamification of ChemDraw during the COVID-19 pandemic: Investigating how a serious, educational-game tournament (molecule madness) impacts student wellness and organic chemistry skills while distance learning. *Journal of Chemical Education*, *97*(9), 3358–3368.

Gran, A. B., Booth, P., & Bucher, T. (2021). To be or not to be algorithm aware: A question of a new digital divide? *Information, Communication & Society*, *24*(12), 1779–1796.

Guaman-Quintanilla, S., Chiluiza, K., Everaert, P., & Valcke, M. (2018). Design thinking in higher education: A scoping review. In *11th annual international conference of education, research and innovation (ICERI)* (pp. 2954–2963). International Academy of Technology, Education and Development (IATED). Seville, Spain.

Guzmán-Valenzuela, C., Gómez-González, C., Rojas-Murphy Tagle, A., & Lorca-Vyhmeister, A. (2021). Learning analytics in higher education: A preponderance of analytics but very little learning? *International Journal of Educational Technology in Higher Education*, *18*, 23.

Han, E. (2022). What is design thinking & why is it important? *HBS Online*. Retrieved from https://online.hbs.edu/blog/post/what-is-design-thinking

Hung, A. C. Y. (2018). Gamification as design thinking. *International Journal of Teaching and Learning in Higher Education*, *30*(3), 549–559.

Kessing, D., & Löwer, M. (2020, October). Work-in-progress: Gamification and design thinking–a motivational analysis of an international, interdisciplinary, team-based university course. In *International conference on interactive collaborative and blended learning* (pp. 65–73). Cham: Springer.

Kim, J., & Castelli, D. M. (2021). Effects of gamification on behavioral change in education: A meta-analysis. *International Journal of Environmental Research and Public Health*, *18*(7), 3550.

Klock, A. C. T., Gasparini, I., Pimenta, M. S., & Hamari, J. (2020). Tailored gamification: A review of literature. *International Journal of Human-Computer Studies*, *144*, 102495.

Krath, J., Schürmann, L., & Von Korflesch, H. F. (2021). Revealing the theoretical basis of gamification: A systematic review and analysis of theory in research on gamification, serious games and game-based learning. *Computers in Human Behavior*, *125*, 106963.

Laundry, L. (2020). What is human-centered design? *HBS Online*. Retrieved from https://online.hbs.edu/blog/post/what-is-human-centered-design

Law, M. P., & Finnigan, J. K. (2021). Letting your students fail: Overcoming failure experiences in undergraduate work-integrated learning. *International Journal of Work-Integrated Learning*, *22*(3), 357–368.

Luka, I. (2019). Design thinking in pedagogy: Frameworks and uses. *European Journal of Education*, *54*(4), 499–512. doi:10.1111/ejed.12367

Mathrani, A., Sarvesh, T., & Umer, R. (2022). Digital divide framework: Online learning in developing countries during the COVID-19 lockdown. *Globalisation, Societies and Education*, *20*(5), 625–640.

Matthews, J., & Wrigley, C. (2017). Design and design thinking in business and management higher education. *Journal of Learning Design*, *10*(1), 41–54.

Muflih, S., Abuhammad, S., Al-Azzam, S., Alzoubi, K. H., Muflih, M., & Karasneh, R. (2021). Online learning for undergraduate health professional education during COVID-19: Jordanian medical students' attitudes and perceptions. *Heliyon*, *7*(9), e08031.

Murillo-Zamorano, L. R., López Sánchez, J. Á., Godoy-Caballero, A. L., & Bueno Muñoz, C. (2021). Gamification and active learning in higher education: Is it possible to match digital society, academia and students' interests? *International Journal of Educational Technology in Higher Education*, *18*, 1–27.

Patrício, R., Moreira, A. C., & Zurlo, F. (2020). Enhancing design thinking approaches to innovation through gamification. *European Journal of Innovation Management*, *24*(5), 1569–1594.

Sahagun, M. A., Moser, R., Shomaker, J., & Fortier, J. (2021). Developing a growth-mindset pedagogy for higher education and testing its efficacy. *Social Sciences & Humanities Open*, *4*(1), 100168.

Sailer, M., & Homner, L. (2020). The gamification of learning: A meta-analysis. *Educational Psychology Review*, *32*, 77–112.

Scheer, A., Noweski, C., & Meinel, C. (2012). Transforming constructivist learning into action: Design thinking in education. *Design and Technology Education*, *17*(3), 8–19.

Villegas, E., Labrador, E., Fonseca, D., Fernández-Guinea, S., & Moreira, F. (2019, July). Design thinking and gamification: User centered methodologies. In *International conference on human-computer interaction* (pp. 115–124). Cham: Springer.

Wolcott, M. D., McLaughlin, J. E., Hubbard, D. K., Rider, T. R., & Umstead, K. (2021). Twelve tips to stimulate creative problem-solving with design thinking. *Medical Teacher*, *43*(5), 501–508.

Zahedi, L., Batten, J., Ross, M., Potvin, G., Damas, S., Clarke, P., & Davis, D. (2021). Gamification in education: A mixed-methods study of gender on computer science students' academic performance and identity development. *Journal of Computing in Higher Education*, *33*(2), 441–474.

Index

achievers 13
active learning, use of 27, 45–46, 48, 54–55
activity based on design thinking, gamification of 63–65; analysis of 66, 71; design and development of 66–67, 71–73; duration of 67, 72; elements of 68, 72; examples of 66–75; implementation and evaluation of 68–71, 73–75; objective of 71; use of gamified platforms 68, 72–73
adaptive gamification 11
adaptive learning 11
analysis of gamified activity 10–15; of future participants 12–15; of Generation Z 12–13; types of learners and 13–15
anxiety 44, 80, 83, 85, 87
artificial intelligence 11
artists 15

Bartle, R. 13
belonging, sense of 55, 83
Blackboard 24, 27, 67
brainstorming 46, 49, 51, 68, 73
broadcasting videoconferences 54

CANVAS model 52, 74
capable benefit seeker 14
capable explorer 14
caring design 87
Center for Curriculum Redesign (CCR) 1, 42
cheating on exams: digital tools for detection of 78; problem of 78
class content, evaluation of 46
ClassDojo platform 24

classroom learning 54
cognitive load theory 9
community building 54–55
constructivist learning theory 9
cooperative learning 46
coopetition 65
corporate training 9
COVID-19 pandemic 7, 24, 52–56, 79; future of higher education after 53; impact of the digital divide on education in developing countries during 79
critical thinking 1, 15, 27, 42, 48
Csíkszentmihályi, M 8–9; flow theory 8–9
cultural differences 78
Curtin, R. 52–55

data integrity 82
David Kelley Design 39
Deci, E. 8
decision-making processes 16, 51, 85
design *see* development of gamified activity
design innovation 39
design thinking 1–2, 9, 28, 55, 70, 80, 86, 87; definition of 39; developmental evaluation as tool for 43; "double diamond" model 40; by drawing on industrial processes 39; ethical issues related to 85, 86–90; examples of 47–52; fundamentals and usefulness of 2; history of 39; human-centered approach in 42–43; in the literature 62–63; meaning of 38–39; method for planning 43–52; models of 39–41;

Index

students learning for the 21st century 41–42; subjective and aesthetic vision of 86; tips for the creation of 88–89; as a tool for the future 55–56; use in higher education 3, 41–43, 51, 55; use of active learning in 45; utility of 40; value of 37; as way of solving problems through innovation 37–38

development of gamified activity 15–25; duration of 22–23; ecological category of 18; elements of 16–17; fictional category of 21–22; performance/measurement category of 17–18; personal category of 20; platforms for 23–25; social category of 18–20

Dichev, C. 14
digital divide 54, 79; concept of 79
digital learning (d-learning) 78
digital literacy, of university teachers 79–80
digital media 10, 24
digital technology 13; availability of devices based on 79; benefits in context of higher education 80; use of 8, 79, 97
distance learning 10, 24
Duggal, K. 8
Duolingo (gamified educational platforms) 24
Dweck, C. 38

"Economics of the European Union" module 48, 66
Economist Intelligence Unit (EIU): "Bridging the Digital Divide to Engage Students in Higher Education" report 53
Educase Review Blog 53
educational app 18
Ekici, M. 17, 26–27, 67
e-learning 11, 26, 78–79; challenges associated with 79
entertainers 14
envy 83
equity, in education 54
ethical issues, related to design thinking 85, 86–90
ethics, in higher education 77–81; associated with the use of digital technology 79; pertaining to privacy and the use of data 81
ethics, in the process of gamification 81–85; literature review of 82; negative side/"darkness" of gamification 82; themes of 82–83
European Centre for the Development of Vocational Training 1, 41
European Union (EU) 1, 41, 47, 49
experiential learning theory 9
exploitation, issue of 83
explorers 13, 14

face-to-face (F2F) time 24, 48–49, 53
flipped classroom methodology, for gamification 26–27, 48, 67, 73, 81
Flipped Learning Network 48
flow theory 8–9

gamification 80; adaptive 11; analysis 10–15; categories of 6–7; classifications of students in 11; creation of user-centered experiences 7; dark side effects of 82–83; definition of 6–8; design and development of 15–25; differences with games 8; educational experience 19; effect on students 6; effects of 12, 19, 22, 26, 84; elements guidance approach 7; ethics and 81–85; familiarization effect 23; goal of 9, 11; implementation and evaluation of 25–26; influence on user motivation and engagement 8, 67; in the literature 62–63; motivational and educational theories of 8–10; negative effects of 83; and other methodologies 26–28; process of 10–26; scenario-based approach 7; technique of 1–2; types of learners *versus* 13–15; use in higher education 6
gamified systems, designers of 22
Generation Y 12
Generation Z 11, 12–13, 66, 79
Ghani, A. 27
Google Forms survey 51, 72, 73, 75
Guaman-Quintanilla, S. 39–40, 43, 96

Hasso Plattner Institute of Design 39–40
higher education 1–2, 21; design
    thinking in 41–43
higher education institutions 53–55
high-impact learning 54

ideaChef tool 62–63
ideation, process of 37
IDEO (international design company)
    39–40, 55; origins of 39
indifferent students 14
individual learning abilities,
    improvement of 81
innovation: design-driven 37; human-
    centered 87; processes of 37;
    solving problems through 37
instructional design 44, 47, 51
interactive games 13
internet, popularization of 78
interpersonal skills 15
intrapersonal intelligence 15
intrinsic motivation 8–9, 19, 22, 86–87
iterative learning cycle 9

Jobs, S. 39

Kahoot (gamified educational platforms)
    24, 27, 67, 72–74, 80
Kelley, D. 39
Khan (gamified educational platforms) 24
killers 13
knowledge acquisition 9, 66
Kolbs' experiential learning theory 9

leaderboards 19, 21–22, 67, 73
leaders 15
learners, types of 14
learning: digital learning (d-learning) 78;
    management systems 24, 63, 67;
    mobile learning (m-learning)
    78; problem-based 46; process
    of 13; project-based 46; social
    nature of 55; *see also specific
    entries*
learning analytics 81
linguistic skills 15
logical-mathematical intelligence 15
luxury industry 18

manipulation, problem of 82
meta-learning 42
Micheli, P. 40
Milanesi, M. 18

Millennials 12
MIT App Inventor 25
mobile data 80
mobile learning (m-learning) 78
Mogavi, H. 84–85
Montreal Declaration 37
Moodle (gamified educational
    platforms) 24
motivation: and ethics of gamification
    82; extrinsic 8; intrinsic 8, 19

naturalistic intelligence 15
new educational technologies, adoption
    of 13, 23

online collaboration tools 48, 50, 52
online job advertisements 1, 41–42
online learning 53–54
oral and written communication 48
out-of-class activities 73–74, 81

participatory learning 45
Philosophy of Technology course 63
plagiarism: committed by university
    students 78; digital tools
    for detection of 78; tools to
    detect 77
plan for design thinking process, in
    higher education 43–52; before
    beginning 43–45; objectives of
    47; planning to Teach 45–46;
    road map of 46–47
problem-solving 1, 41, 43, 46, 87; by
    process of design thinking 38;
    through innovation 37
project-based learning 27–28
proprietary gamified platform 25
prototyping, issue of 46, 52
psychological safety 89, 98
psychological well-being 85

Quizbot 24
Quizziz (gamified educational
    platforms) 24

remote learning 53–55
renovation 20
researchers 15
"Rethinking College Admissions"
    project 55
Robinson, K. 41
Rodrigues, L. 22–23, 67, 72
role-playing activity 50

Index

role playing exercises 50, 69–70
Ryan, R. M. 8

self-determination theory 8–9
self-recrimination 85
social interaction 13, 19, 70, 89, 98
socializers 13, 15
social networks, use of 19–20
Socrative 24
Stanford d.school model 40, 46–48, 66, 97
Stanford University 39, 43; Hasso Plattner Institute of Design 40
storyboard 50, 52, 70
storytelling 21, 88
strategic learners 15
struggling benefit seeker 14
struggling explorer 14
student motivation, influence exerted by gamification on 67
students' technological skills, development of 79
surveillance and privacy 82–83

SWOT (strengths, weaknesses, opportunities, threats) analysis 50, 52, 71, 75

task identity 79
teacher training 42–43, 51
technical knowledge 25, 48, 66
testers 15
Toda, A. M. 17–19, 21, 65
tutoring, student-adapted 42

university students, effects of gamification on 26–27

value creation 7, 37
Verganti, R. 2, 37
video games 85; online multiplayer games 13
virtual learning 13, 23
vocational education and training 41

WhatsApp 19

Zondle 24

For Product Safety Concerns and Information please contact our EU representative GPSR@taylorandfrancis.com
Taylor & Francis Verlag GmbH, Kaufingerstraße 24, 80331 München, Germany

www.ingramcontent.com/pod-product-compliance
Lightning Source LLC
Chambersburg PA
CBHW051757230426
43670CB00012B/2322